Zodiac, Crystals and Moon Rituals

Written by Nina Lekic, a beautiful soul from the Moon
Omens Family. Created by the collective efforts of
the Moon Omens Family with the sole purpose of helping
you remember who you truly are and to help you step
back into your infinite divine power.

Table of Contents

Introduction to Crystals and Astrology

Crystals and astrology have been tightly connected since ancient times and have always been used for healing, gaining wisdom, receiving insights, self-discovery, spirituality, and self-mastery. People have used crystals for centuries; we're now rediscovering this knowledge that our ancestors knew and practiced since forever. Since a long time ago—since the mythical lost city of Atlantis and even further back, through all civilizations, in the legendary cities of Mu, Hyperborea, and Asgard—our ancestors have used crystals and astrology in spiritual rituals and for physical healing. They were communicating with nature and everything around and within it. Many mythical stories tell us that certain deities were born in stone. In prehistoric times, people used stones as tools and weapons. They used these tools for powerful expansion of all sources of energies—physical, mental, emotional, and spiritual.

Crystals are gifts of our divine Mother Nature; they are specific keys to the Universe. They are magical keepers of energy and they possess live energy that has a beneficial influence on human organisms. Their gracious and generous energy and influence have been known and appreciated forever. The magic of crystals belongs to natural, organic, and pure magic. It belongs to the magic of elements and the language of mysteries; it is not something that is beyond our reach. It is a gift to us humans from our Mother Nature who embraces matter and spirit together. It is a gift to us to use this magic and to help ourselves, gain wisdom, and learn things that are beyond our logical, intellectual understanding. Crystals possess certain codes through frequencies that correspond with our human nature. Their vibrations are in direct resonance with our being, and they work in our favor. These magical

1

stones emanate benevolent energies which are soothing and grounding for us. They are all different and hold different energies; each crystal is unique and has its own vibration, color, thickness, number, quality, and influence. Each crystal represents a specific vibrant key that serves as a decoder for wrong beliefs, twisted perceptions, traumas, mental and emotional blockages, and self-destructive patterns.

Crystals have multilayered influences. They are live beings, and each of them has a certain role. They are connected with Christ consciousness, which has nothing to do with church and religion, only with pure awareness and awakening. The name of Christ is coded and keeps secrets of awakening and coming to consciousness. Crystals and Christ are also connected with the Krishna deity in Hinduism. They all hold the same roots in their names; they also have the cross in common. The cross represents four elements and their unity in human beings. The horizontal line of the cross represents matter and energy. Matter is the earth element, and energy belongs to the element of water. The vertical line of the cross represents time and space. Time equals the element of air, and space, the element of fire. The horizontal and vertical lines are intertwined and form a cross. Ether embraces all of these elements, and crystals and astrology are keepers of this wisdom.

In astrology, there are twelve signs in the Zodiac, and each sign belongs to one of these four elements. Using crystals and astrology together is very strong and powerful because it transforms lives, and it is extremely useful for our inner journey. We can heal and transform our own energies using the healing properties from these elements and through the knowledge of astrology and crystals. The purpose of this magic is to improve personal vitality and inner strength, enhance feelings of love for life and nature, develop feelings and taste for beauty, receive insights that help us and support us on our life path, and harmonize our individual nature with cosmic rhythms.

Crystals can be used or misused—it all depends on who uses them and in whose hands the crystals lie. They can be used for gaining power over things and people, but this is not the way to use them because they are very strong. This won't lead you toward light and awakening, but rather eventually toward self-destruction. It is very important to use crystals with pure intention and a pure heart.

Each crystal influences each person in a different way. There are many crystals on this beautiful planet Earth, and there are plenty for everyone. Each crystal vibrates and emanates differently, and Mother Nature took care of creating these patterns in the most beautiful and magnificent way.

These minerals are alive. They hold life within their structure; they have always fascinated human beings, especially because of their hypnotic visual performances. Minerals are capable of interacting and reacting with the light because of their specific structure. The atoms in a crystal form a virtual three-dimensional grid. This atomic grid of crystals follows seven basic geometric shapes: triangle, square, rectangle, hexagon, rhomboid, parallelogram, and trapezium. As the crystal grows, these basic shapes of the grid get multiplied, and through this multiplying of the crystal grid, we get pyramidal shapes, and so on.

No matter in which shape crystals appear, they have one thing in common: the ability to transmit light. Crystals can refract the rays of light, which is how they become charged with energy. Light can be reflected, scattered, or refracted by the crystal. Crystals can be programmed by absorbing energies, and they have a powerful ability to store huge amounts of information, which makes them essential tools within high technology usage.

Listen to crystals. Listen to what they tell you; they will teach you how to read symbols and subtle messages. Return to them positive energy in the same manner as they emanate love and light to you. Crystals receive energy from our thoughts and emotions, so working with crystals and stars demands our participation and conscious involvement. We have to be aware of what we want to achieve, release, receive, and transform. We become the active co-creators that we truly are in our essence, and that is our mission—that each and every one of us becomes a co-creator with life and Source. Once you start working with crystals and astrology, you will soon start noticing how things start coming to you at the right time. Valuable information and messages will start appearing, and crystals that are perfect for that period of time for you and your life will come to you. Synchronicity becomes more evident, and you'll have an ability to see it and read it.

Crystals emit, generate, and absorb vibrations and energies. Crystals receive, keep, and return frequencies that are sent to them. They respond to the wearer in an appropriate manner, so if you keep your intentions pure and send positive vibrations to your crystal, it will answer by increasing that purity and optimism.

Crystals interact and communicate with our consciousness, subconsciousness, nervous and cellular systems, glands, DNA, and chakras. They can be placed on certain parts of the body where we feel the pain or anxiety and on chakras to activate these centers and untie knots that prevent the free flow of energy through our system.

Instructions for How to Use and Read This Book

Astrology and crystals can truly transform lives if used in the right way and if there's true dedication involved from our part as human beings. We are not our sun sign only; we are much more than that. We are much more than our Zodiac, but we have to go through the wheel to experience stories and pass exams. We have to learn lessons, gain wisdom, clear karmic patterns, and release ourselves from limitations. Unlocking each level of the Zodiac wheel within us will help us awaken true powers of each sign through ourselves. We are all given a unique natal chart print at birth, which is our bill we came here with. This chart helps us to discover and reveal what our mission is, why we experience certain issues, what our gifts are, where we fail, what our sensitive spots are, what makes us angry, what makes us happy, which archetypes live through us, what we need to do to develop and improve, and what we need to get rid of. All these characteristics, personalities, and identities show us which cards are given to us to play with, and it is up to us how we will use them. We can self-heal and help ourselves and others on many levels. We are given these tools to get to know ourselves better, to learn about nature, to communicate with our inner world, and get in touch with the Source and divine.

Through these pages, you are given a guide and information on how to heal and nurture your physical, emotional, and mental states and how to get closer to your spirit and soul. As we have said, we are much more than our sun sign, and astrology is not deterministic, as many see and perceive it. On the contrary, it shows us that we have our free will, that we can change and transform our destiny and karma, that we are given this power to break from our cells, to free ourselves from imprisonment of attachments. We are hooked on everything. We get attached so easily and completely forget our true nature, identifying ourselves with our addictions and attachments. We start believing that we are those things, and we get stuck. We tend to repeat ourselves, and we can hardly imagine doing things differently. That's why most of us never get a chance to get out of that closed system that is self-created through habits, attachments, routines, and beliefs that won't let our perception change. This is how we get stuck and hardly achieve any big transformation through life. Astrology actually shows us the way to break free, learn lessons constructively, and gain true knowledge. With astrology, we can learn how to experience life from all sides, experiment with ourselves and our lives, and be more open to new things, changes, and transformations. Astrology teaches us that certain things are meant to be, but mostly we have our free will to choose what we do with life and how we feel about it.

For the most accurate perception and vision of yourself, you should read your ascendant sign, your sun sign, and your moon sign. These will give you a clearer vision and fuller image of yourself. They will show you in a more valid way your past, childhood, issues, traumas, present life, and issues that you confront daily. They can show you repetitive patterns and things that you keep experiencing that can help you understand yourself more intimately.

You might want to search for your dominant sign, which many times turns out to be one of these three signs: sun, moon, or ascendant. It also may be another sign completely, so it is advisable to read also for your dominant sign. If you want to find out which sign is dominant in your natal chart, we will explain this at the end of this chapter under the title, "How to Find Out Which Sign Dominates Your Natal Chart."

When doing meditations and rituals, no matter which sign you are, you can use your journal and write down your experiences. Write down all the things you find worth mentioning. You can write down your wishes and intentions on a piece of paper before or after your meditation. You can play music with healing frequencies and use incense, smudge sticks, palo santo, or any other medium to purify your space. You can do something that resonates with you the most. These meditations are not strict, and you are not obliged to follow any rules. Feel free to experiment because this is what it's all about. You should become more liberated and free to meet your potential and your gifts, to discover things that make you feel good, to find out what you want and what comforts you and also to find out what distracts you, what hurts you, what makes you feel anxious, and what damages you. You should feel free to use any technique you want to make yourself feel good and comfortable.

Use these pages to navigate yourself and find the answers within yourself. Use these pages to inspire you and motivate you, to awaken your true self, to start loving yourself and appreciating your life. Use these pages to initiate self-betterment. Lose what is not yours and discover what is truly yours; let go of your possessions, attachments, unhealthy relationships, self-destructive thoughts and emotions, damaging habits, and all things that prevent you from transforming and self-developing. You are always growing, and you should remember that through every moment. Remember that you, a human being, are a work in progress. You are constantly growing and maturing, and you are an infinite eternal being. You are powerful and mighty; you have all the elements of existence within you, and you are a microworld. You contain everything that exists within you, and you should work toward making this truth become conscious within you. You should work toward reminding yourself of this every minute of every day. This is also a great part of inner work—reminding yourself of who you truly are.

Keep yourself awake and aware as much as you can through every single thing that you're doing, feeling, thinking, saying, writing, and dreaming. Be more aware of every move you make, every bite you taste, every sip you drink, every word you speak, every emotion you send and receive, every deed you make, every action you take, every breath you take in and out, every step you walk, everything you touch, smell, see and hear, and everything you observe around you and within you. Work toward making it all crystal clear. Raise your awareness and be present; try to practice this whenever you're into it and whenever you remember doing it. Acknowledge it and comprehend it. Feel yourself and start feeling things and people more. This will help you tremendously and will transform your life.

Affirmations are beautiful and efficient tools to keep yourself uplifted and remind yourself of your connection with everything that exists. You can read and use affirmations that are written through these pages for any sign you want, and you can use your own affirmations, too. Maybe those in these pages will inspire you to create your own individual and authentic affirmations.

You can also use meditations from these pages for all signs with your own crystal. It doesn't matter if you have a Taurus crystal and you want to do a Capricorn meditation. You can also use these meditations while there's a new or full moon in certain signs. For example, if you are a Gemini and there's a new moon happening in Scorpio, you can meditate to the Scorpio new moon meditation for that day. Or, if there's a full moon in Cancer, go through the full moon Cancer meditation. Feel free to experiment. You can also use these meditations on a regular day, before or after new and full moons. This can inspire you to find your own ways of meditating and contemplating so that you can meet with your intuition and become a true co-creator of reality. Remember, you create what you intend.

How to Find Out Which Sign Dominates Your Natal Chart

It is very simple to find out your dominant sign in the natal chart. Follow the steps below or go to this link to check the video on how to do it:

https://www.youtube.com/watch?v=IEz1-H47n4s

Go to astro.com.

Find the tab **Free Horoscopes**, look for the last section **Drawings & Calculations**, and choose **Extended Chart Selection**.

Enter your birth data if you haven't already.

Above the Natal Chart Wheel box are sections in tabs called Round, Special, Ephemeris, and Pullen/Astrolog. Choose the last one called **Pullen/Astrolog**.

Open the dropbox for **Chart Type** and choose the last option called **Simple Chart Delineation by Walter Pullen**. Click to show the chart.

Scroll all the way down until you see a table with planets, signs, and percentages. It could be easier if you just search on the page for the word "percent." Just type Ctrl+f and enter the word "percent" in the box. It will take you to the table of dominant signs and planets. Here you can check which planet is the most dominant by looking under the Percent column. You can also look for the number 1 under the Rank column and see which planet or sign is dominant. You can also check in the same place which element—fire, earth, air, or water—rules you the most.

Crystals and the Zodiac

ARIES

Aries Sacred Stones and Rituals

Aries is the first sign of the Zodiac and the first fire sign. Aries rules the head, brain, and eyes, and these body parts should always be taken extra care of. These are strong and sensitive parts at the same time. The first consideration is your motivation. You are born with the affirmation I AM; you have fire as a ruling element, and you struggle with patience and self-control. Aries is alpha and omega, the spark which initiates new birth. You are prone to accidents and injuries because you have fiery impulses moving you to take action; your reactions are fast and often without thinking, which usually causes destructive behavior and situations. You strongly identify with your body and personality, which is why you passionately defend yourself and feel threatened by your surroundings. You are the daring one. Being the first and made of fire makes you an initiator and a pioneer. You start things and bring new and fresh enthusiasm wherever you appear. You possess enormous vital energy and physical strength, and you can quickly get angry and react in unpredictable ways. You have an amazing will, and you want to get things done.

You are independent and have a hard time channeling wild sparks that quickly burst into flames and leave you feeling exhausted and frustrated. You should learn to surf those wildfires. You are distracted by so many things, and you struggle to deal with excitement. You are often under tension, and it is of the utmost importance for you to train how to relax. You have to keep your head cool and keep your body free from stress and toxins. You go through a lot of conflicting outer experiences, which ultimately bring you wisdom of knowing when the perfect time is to use that extreme force and how to properly and constructively direct your fearless nature. You have enormous strength and willingness. You won't settle until you achieve what you have on your mind. You can be extremely stubborn, which brings you many obstacles on your life path, but which also motivates you to get things done and finish what you have started. You initiate new activities and new beginnings; you have the power to break from the past, to liberate from boundaries, to get rid of old ways of doing things. You are always ready.

You need excitement and stimulation almost all the time, you need your adrenaline satisfied, and this is all part of the process that leads you toward greater self-discoveries and self-development. But you can become stuck in this adrenaline and rush addiction, which can make you feel like you're always missing something in life. You often need that extreme feeling of being alive and being on the edge of something.

Your sign is represented by the rebirth of the sun in the spring after the dark of the winter. This always motivates you to go through life and lifts up your will to move forward. You have this potential to conquer the darkness and fake light. You can emanate true light, but first you have to experience going through the ego trap in order to master your lessons and yourself. Your drive and passions are very high. Your vital energy is strong, and this gives you great abilities to fight through life and never give up. Still, you can get yourself into a lot of unnecessary fights when you act directly from the unconscious and immature ego and that fake light of having to be right, always putting yourself before others,

14

competing and comparing with others, and having the need to be the first and the best. These desires are not bad in their essence because they keep you alive. Being affirmative and persistent and willing is amazing, but when these things come from the need to defeat others, to prove yourself in something, to dominate in any way, to show that you're better than this or that, than him or her, than them and the whole world, then these things can come to you as a boomerang; you become a magnet for troubles and fights.

In your journey of learning lessons, you often spill and waste a lot of strength just to prove yourself and express your feelings. You want quick results. You have to master these fiery waves and become aware of your huge capacities; you need to acknowledge what these energies truly mean and how to manifest them in a healthy way so that you really become your own master and get to know who you are. You will be able to meet your identity and body and enhance your abilities of creating new things and purifying the heart.

Crystals hold exquisite powers to help you heal your wounds, improve your natural gifts, and overcome your weaknesses. Working with crystals will help you get rid of tensions, unhealthy anger, traumas, and toxic desires. It will bring you relief and unlock your potential. They can help tremendously with releasing any damaging mind and body patterns, getting you closer to your true expressions and creative talents, waking up your spirituality, and connecting you to the wisdom of knowing what is right and what is wrong. You will receive wisdom for making the right decisions, mastery of controlling your impatience, and your full potential of influencing others.

Crystals help you through life to get yourself in order, help yourself, heal your wounds, and transform things for the better. It really is incredible. When you use crystals consciously, you can become closer with your own energy and yourself in general. They bring you closer to nature as well and introduce you to a new way of living your life. You can get more harmony within yourself and inner peace; you will move closer to a more fulfilled life and true adventures that satisfy your needs and bring you wisdom of seeing through things. Crystals can truly change your life for the better, and they will bring you important answers.

Crystals that are in resonance with you, Aries, that reflect your energy in the best way and awaken and charge your warrior spirit, are carnelian, citrine, ruby, amethyst, bloodstone, emerald, garnet, rose quartz, aquamarine, red jasper, and diamond.

The one crystal that gives you the best connection with your inner and outer existence is carnelian.

Carnelian

Carnelian is perfect for you, dear Aries. It encourages you and gives you healthier self-confidence. It is a red-orange crystal that resonates very well with your ruling planet Mars and its warm energy. It provides deeper intimacy with your identity. At the same time, it absorbs excessive and unused energy and gives it back when needed. It reconnects you with your body, empowering endurance and protection. It awakens your true warrior spirit from within; it activates your cells to work in order and to be in sync with your outer actions and achievements. It helps you use physical vital energy productively; it helps you with your physical training and martial arts, exercises, and coordination, bringing body energy levels to work properly. It helps you attract success and encourages you to overcome instability and impatience. It protects you from accidents and pressures from your surroundings. Carnelian is also connected with love and passion; it holds passive and active codes that work in accordance with the awareness of the one who uses it. It perfectly matches your Aries moods and cleanses accumulated toxins. It is a fertility and potency crystal as well, so it can be used to enliven these potentials in you and to remove difficulties of not knowing what to do with your energy and vitality.

Carnelian restores lost strength and improves concentration, which is very important for you, Aries. It helps you maintain great self-stability and control, and it stimulates your creativity and protects you from your or someone else's rage. It gives you stabilization and removes feelings of jealousy and possessive behavior. Carnelian recovers your purpose on Earth and feelings of lost identity, and it rebuilds independence and freedom. It has a dual nature, since it is a fiery and passionate crystal, but at the same time, it is a grounding and protective stone. It was believed to calm the blood. It is a yang stone, which recharges your vitality, creativity, and life energy. It makes you less vulnerable to outside circumstances and protects you from negative influences of all kinds. It helps you achieve sexual balance and restore your vital organs. It has a healing effect on your lower chakras and sends warming energy toward them.

Carnelian improves your libido, and it's great for any issues with the reproductive system. It is connected with your sacral chakra, and it stimulates her opening and balancing. It heals issues with your root chakra. It helps you become comfortable with your skills and talents; it makes you use your individuality in the best possible way. It stimulates the first three chakras.

Carnelian promotes huge passion, creative energy, and strong courage. It inspires you in your artistic expressions. It reminds you of your talents and helps you express and manifest your hidden gifts. It brings great assertive will and encourages you to stop waiting for the miracles to happen, to take a risk and make a move toward manifesting your dreams. It reminds you that your body is a temple and makes you aware that you need to maintain healthy physical conditions. It helps you get still and inspires you to work actively on your self-discovery. It has a purifying effect and enables you to work effectively on self-control. It has a calming effect on anger and reconnects you with your inner sight of recognizing the right moment for action. It is a perfect crystal for you to become who you are supposed to be, to open the path of playing the true role of your life and to know who you are behind that role so that you can play it and enjoy it fully.

Citrine

Citrine is excellent for success and wealth, but it has many other purposes. It can be used for healing the body, mind, and spirit. Its name comes from the Latin *citrina*, which is associated with its pale-yellow color; citrine was once called the "Sun Stone," its color was connected with gold, and it was also called the "Merchant's Stone." It is also known as the "Money Stone" because it was thought to bring great prosperity. It helps you overcome depression, heal traumas, reveal inner issues, release anger, and improve communication skills. It is perfect for manifesting and creating. It is associated with the solar plexus chakra, and it is a powerful healing stone. It regenerates and purifies. It carries the power of the sun and is warming and energizing. Citrine transmutes negative energies; it also absorbs and grounds any unwanted and damaging vibrations. It helps you release your wounds and scars and is an empowering stone that removes any tendencies toward destructive behavior, thoughts, words, and emotions. It activates your imagination and rejuvenates your creativity. It brings you mental clarity and helps you get to the source of an issue. It is great for manifestations and new beginnings. It is also good for bringing intelligence, happiness, health, curiosity, and confidence. Citrine can help in accepting criticism, and it brings more understanding. It helps with clearing energetic blockages. It holds strong positive vibrations and brings mind illumination.

Ruby

Ruby is a red stone that goes well with red Mars energy and your natural energy. It is great for physical strength and vitality, and it increases life force energy, endurance, and positive thoughts. It removes feelings of exhaustion; it helps you overcome laziness and lethargy. It can be used for healing wounds and revitalization. It reconnects you with youth and fresh new energy. It is also useful for any kind of competition or promotion because it brings strong determination. It promotes leadership skills, which are natural to you. It has a calming effect on hyperactivity and dispels any self-destructive tendencies. It encourages you to follow your bliss and makes you feel worthy of love. It stimulates your base chakra and attracts healthy sexual activities.

Ruby encourages true passion liberated from aggression. It improves your motivation and encourages you to speak the truth for those who are threatened or who are being falsely accused. It helps you overcome dependencies and emotional attachments; it helps you understand your relationships with others and dispels doubts. It is a very encouraging stone that infuses you with enormous strength and endurance while inspiring you to get things going. It detoxifies your body and is good for your circulatory system and heart. It makes you appreciate your physical body and it also detoxifies your blood. It stimulates the pineal gland and truly inspires you to be who you're born to be.

Amethyst

Amethyst holds intense energies; it is an extremely powerful stone with a very strong energetic field. It is known as a stone for meditation and it is perfect for metaphysical use. It heightens spiritual knowledge and experiences; it stimulates the mind and brings clarity of visions and thoughts. It brings sobriety on a physical and a metaphysical level. It helps you get rid of addictions of all kinds, be it food, sex, drugs, alcohol, worst-case-scenario patterns, or any damaging habit you hold on to. It cleanses your blood and boosts your immunity. It brings you calmness and helps you get out of chaos and confusion. It brings you deeper understanding and inspires you to act through spiritual knowledge and higher guidance.

Amethyst helps you gain more balance and channel ambitions in a productive way. It is great for accessing inner-self realms and doing the self-healing process. It releases you from stress and anxiety and awakens intuition while calming your mind. It protects you from harm and liberates you from temptations. Amethyst brings you peace of mind and calms your fears; it keeps you undisturbed. It is a perfect stone for connecting with your higher self. It is connected with your crown chakra, and it merges you with realms beyond the physical world. It helps you identify damaging patterns and imbalances. It protects you from nightmares and is helpful with insomnia issues.

Bloodstone

Bloodstone is a type of jasper. It is a heliotrope also known as "Sun Stone" or "Christ Stone." It is your stone of courage and has been connected with Aries throughout the ages. Bloodstone restores your physical and metaphysical abilities and strengths, it protects you from deception, and it has detoxing qualities. It brings clarity and links your root and heart chakras, bringing them into balance. It's used for self-awareness and protects you from threats. It motivates you to achieve your goals. It promotes courage and is a powerful healing and purifying stone.

Bloodstone cleanses the auric field and brings you feelings of wholeness, unity, and balance. It is a powerful grounding stone too. It stimulates your root chakra and grounds you completely. It brings you great strength and determination. It is perfect for new beginnings and fresh starts; it also helps you to proceed and continue what you have started. It is a great motivator. It gives you courage to move on no matter what, it supports you through life despite obstacles and troubles, it helps you to not give up. It is connected with energies of Mars and blood. It is said it purifies the blood. It awakens your inner warrior energies and great self-control abilities.

Emerald

Emerald is a prosperity stone. It provides great hope and improves memory and intelligence. It is great for renewals and emotional well-being. It calms the troubled mind and brings faith and inner peace. It develops psychic powers and prevents infections and diseases. It offers uplifting energy and it's connected with heart chakra, bringing balance to relationships with friends and lovers. It is a stone of infinite patience and it is known as a stone of successful love.

According to a legend, emerald comes from the Sanskrit word *Marakata*, which means "the green of things that grow." Its name transformed gradually through time and it is an ancient stone of magic and mystery. It promotes unconditional love, hope, encouragement, and abundance. It symbolizes youth, vitality, renewal, and regeneration. It offers you great protection from all kinds of spells or black magic. It is known as the revealer of the truth. It eliminates negativity and strengthens your heart. It is a wisdom stone and it enhances truth, clarity, and clear communication. It increases psychic abilities. It encourages you to enjoy life and to open up to divine energies.

Garnet

Garnet is the traditional stone of Aries. It's the vitality stone known as a stone of health. It purifies energies. It activates the survival instinct mode and offers courage, strength and success. It's a mind opening stone and it sharpens your perception. It increases self-confidence and stimulates your metabolism. Garnet is great for boosting your immune system and restoring the will to live. It improves life quality and removes obstacles, it dispels depression. It re-energizes your body and your chakras, it awakens the passionate fire within you, it stimulates kundalini rising energy.

Garnet enhances your sexuality, creativity, and vitality. It makes you aware of your individual responsibility and personal freedom that comes along with it. It has grounding qualities and it is also known as a stone of commitment. It helps you understand your true desires and goals. It helps you deal with challenging situations. It boosts your life force and helps you dissolve outdated patterns from your life.

Rose Quartz

Rose quartz has gentle and nourishing energy and it benefits you, dear Aries, in dealing with aggression and imbalances. It brings selflessness and awakens self-love free from judgments. It has great power in healing processes and it provides unconditional love and emotional healing. It brings feelings of peace and harmony and helps in dealing with losses and traumas. It awakens empathy and rebuilds trust.

Rose quartz is a stone of infinite peace and pure love. It is an essential stone for the heart chakra, and it teaches you the true meaning of love, love for yourself, your close ones, your family, nature, the planets, the whole existence. It enhances empathy, compassion, forgiveness, and the awakening of the heart. It allows you to deeply connect with others, to link your heart to the hearts of others. It has a strong healing influence and it eases and cures feelings of grief and despair. It brings you healing of heart issues. It attracts love and helps you release unexpressed emotions from the past.

Aquamarine

Aquamarine is a great stone to cool down your head when you feel too fiery. It helps you to tame the flames. It quiets your mind and reduces tension. It brings you more tolerance for others and it clears confusion. It is very good for self-expression which is important for you, Aries, and it brings more flexibility within your actions and thoughts. It provides more freedom, moving you beyond limitations.

Aquamarine is connected with the throat chakra and allows you to speak clearly and truthfully. It inspires you to speak from your heart and to speak the truth. It encourages gentle communication, intellectual growth, spiritual knowledge, and intuition. It is also known as the stone of release. It helps you find quick solutions to any problem. It helps you discover emotional patterns that prevent your spiritual growth and allows you to heal from them. It supports the release of old attachments and it brings you great strength to deal with grieving. It promotes tolerance and helps you overcome a judgmental attitude. It calms feelings of fear and worry and connects you with your innermost truth.

Red Jasper

Red jasper is a very protective stone and is extremely beneficial for you. It gives you the ability to think before acting. It grounds your energy and brings tranquility, it cleanses your body and detoxifies your blood. This stone brings issues out on the surface in order to heal them and let them go. It brings feelings of compassion and completion.

This crystal is an amazing grounding stone and it enormously helps you to engage with the world and accept external circumstances and influences. It is a powerful stabilizing stone and it stimulates your root chakra. It is a great stone for regression therapies. It activates sexual energies and manifesting energies. It deeply connects you to the energies of the earth and brings you greater understanding of nature. It makes you aware of the magical connection between Human and Nature. It brings you insights about the most difficult situations in life, it strengthens you and stabilizes your aura. Red Jasper motivates you and pushes you to become the person you truly are. It reminds you of your true origin and your essential self. It is also known as a "supreme nurturer."

Diamond

Diamond is the most durable of all gemstones. It has the life force energy of the sun and it brings you purity and clarity. It offers you perfection in all actions, it helps you while you struggle with challenges, it brings growth and a higher state of consciousness, it reconnects you with your true self. It's a great stone for making commitments and gaining self-discipline; it brings feelings of invincibility and makes you achieve structure and endurance. It allows your soul to shine and it brings you enlightenment. Diamond revitalizes your brain functions.

It is a symbol of faithfulness, innocence, purity, and love. It helps you if you feel lost or confused, it brings your mind, body, and emotions into alignment. It cleanses your aura from negativity and activates your crown chakra. Diamond will magnify your emotions and act as a mirror to your emotional state, so it is important to wear this crystal consciously knowing that it will increase your emotions whether they're positive or negative. It is a stone of fulfillment and it brings your wishes and dreams into reality. It enhances your creativity and imagination and increases self-worth and self-love. It brings you feelings of inner peace and calmness.

New and Full Moon Rituals Using Carnelian

Carnelian can be used in different practices, rituals, and meditations. During the moon phases, its powers are enhanced and aligned with the universal tides, connecting cosmic energy flows with the initiator of the ritual.

As an Aries, your strength, willingness, and confidence magnify the powers of carnelian and make them work for you. Using carnelian during new and full moon cycles is extremely advisable because it makes you use the full potential of the energies that surround you. Meditation is supremely powerful with carnelian during the moon phases for you and it can cleanse your energies in unimaginable ways. You can achieve many things that you thought were impossible. Your intentions become seeds which come to fruition. You start receiving remarkable insights about your past and your future. You can release many things from your inner self and new perceptions of reality become available for you. You can unlock mental and emotional blockages and transform your life on many levels.

Having fire as your ruling element, you can light a candle and cleanse and recharge your gemstone by bringing it close to the flame and setting your pure intentions. You can also run it through smoke while smudging with a palo santo stick or incense. Carnelian can be cleansed under clear water once a week and it is not advisable to use saltwater.

New Moon

The new moon is a time to plant a seed for growth, to start something new, and visualize that dream you have. It is creative energy and marks new beginnings. When you have your sacred stone cleansed and activated by your intention and candlelight, you can energize it with your body by holding it in your hand or placing it somewhere on your body where you feel you need it the most. You can either sit in a position you feel comfortable or you can lay on the floor and just relax. You should keep your intention focused while sending it to your stone.

You start feeling energy circulating from your head to the gem, and you can visualize that electricity and vibrations as a constant flow between your spirit, your body, and the crystal. Focus on your breathing and as you inhale, feel the codes of light from the carnelian being sent to your whole body, inhale that light, and as you exhale, send all the tension and blockages that you feel. It will receive it and transform it into new and refreshed energy. This detoxifies your energy field and body toxins and gives you renewed forces, which make you fresh and clean and available and open for making your intention manifest.

Remember, your crystal is alive. It listens to you and your intentions, so make sure your intention is coming from the heart instead of egoic wishes and desires. You should use this time of the new moon phase and your crystal to reconnect with cosmic energies and start something that truly resonates with you. Set your intentions for some great new goal, that job you love doing, the love you know you deserve, a healthy body, healthy daily habits, a new way of life, inner strength, self-control, more understanding of yourself and others, awakening of your true potentials which are still asleep and you're not aware of them yet, whatever you know you need and deserve, whatever you want to achieve for self-betterment and the betterment of those around you. Enjoy your ritual, enjoy the ride.

Make a list of your wishes during the new moon phase. Write down as many wishes as your inspiration can create. Don't force it. You can read them out loud after you're done writing them down, or you can just imagine and envision all of them, or you can do all of this. You can burn this paper after your ritual is done if you feel like it, or you can put it in some sacred space of yours, you can put a crystal on your wish paper and meditate on it. Feel free to experiment as long as you have pure intentions.

New Moon Aries Affirmations

I choose spirit as my authority
I respect others' wishes
I hold myself down without holding myself back
I allow new beginnings to come to me
I awaken my divine nature
I have... (write down whatever it is that you wish to have)
I choose healthy habits
I make decisions which are best for me and people around me
I acknowledge my feelings and thoughts easily
I awaken an inner warrior
I create exactly what I need

I trust in the process
I know that where I am now is leading me to where I want to be
I honor myself and who I am in this very moment without wanting to
be anyone else
I honor my lessons
I accept myself fully

Full Moon

The full moon is that period of time when you have an opportunity to get rid of something that has been a burden, to free yourself from pent-up emotions. It is time for release, time to get free of everything that's holding you back or weighing you down. Working with your crystal on the full moon amplifies these liberations and clears the path from the root to the roof so you can unfold your manifestations free of disturbances and obstacles along the way.

For you, Aries, the energy of the full moon is a magical time to work on your freedom, to use that fire and burn away whatever's no longer needed. Your desires and passions are not something you have to remove from yourself, and that is not possible. These sacred forces are there so you can use them constructively; impatience can be turned into getting things done quickly, and anger can be used to channel it through breaking something that is rotten and used up. Everything has its purpose, and under the full moon you have an opportunity to sink into the cosmic wisdom and download knowledge of using these integrated powers in a true way.

You can use your crystal just by wearing it and feeling it on your skin. Get into connection with it, speak with it, say what it is you no longer need and offer it to leave. Ask for wisdom and understanding of your fire. You can dance it away, you may dance with music you find comfortable for you, or in silence just following your inner rhythm. You can do it as long as you wish, no limitations, just dance and let yourself be swept away by your moves, feel your physical body and charge that feeling of being a magician of your life. Allow the energy to work through you free of mind and body twists. Dance until you feel your body is light and easy, dance until you forget about everything that is causing you harm or any kind of guilt or anger. When your dance is done, sit or lie down, feel your body and just let yourself be as long as you enjoy it. Feel yourself calm as a lake and let the magnetic powers of the moon attract and take away what you feel free to let go of. Feel your mind and body restored and renewed. Light that fire of yours with new impulses. Resurrect yourself.

Full Moon Aries Affirmations

I have courage to heal myself
I own my ambitions and give them meaning
I realign with my purpose
I take risks to become my own best version
I have control of seeing my actions and reactions before manifesting them
I let go of impulsiveness and anger
I remember who I am
I respond to the divine
I release my hatred and frustrations
I deal with my fears effectively
I let go of destructive patterns
I am aware of my own powers
I choose personal freedom
I forgive everyone who has wronged me and most importantly,
I forgive myself
I release all that's not in alignment with my highest good
I attract people and places that resonate with my truth

TAURUS

Taurus Sacred Stones and Rituals

Taurus belongs to the earth element and rules the throat, neck, and vocal cords. That's why these parts of the body are physically and metaphysically strong and sensitive at the same time. This makes your voice memorable and strong; you literally create and manifest with it. You can be a great singer, you are multitalented in all branches of art, you are musical and can be a true virtuoso in fine arts. Because it's the first sign of the earth triad in the Zodiac, Taurus ruled by Venus represents embodiment. Mother Earth in all its wild and sensual nature and glory is connected with Taurus. That's why you are strongly connected with the body and form, beauty and shapes, and manifestations in the physical world. You represent an eruption of primordial instincts and perseverance at the same time. You enjoy and honor abundance. The quality and quantity of things are of the same importance to you. You develop deep attachments to material possessions which can make you possessive and attached, unable to let go of what you own. Taurus holds the I HAVE principle and symbolizes the matrix of this world as well as the womb of the cosmos.

Your earthly nature can make you pretty stubborn in your way of thinking and doing, and it's hard for you to adjust in new and sudden situations. It's not easy for you to accept changes. You strive to bring and achieve stability and consistency; you need to feel your emotional and material worlds secured. You want to keep things the way they are once you get that feeling of security, you want to have it constantly, you want continuity. You have a very strong and determined will, which pushes you to endure and withstand everything that comes to you. You handle hard times as a true stoic, but this tendency can also lead you to get sick and to damage your body. You need to learn to have more trust and faith, to learn to let go easily, to get more flexible and break your fixed nature bit by bit. You need to master your own potential, to gain wisdom of knowing how to use endurance and persistence in a constructive and useful way. You possess great power of fertility, strength, and fortitude. You are often led by your desires and you can easily become a victim of them if you let them guide you unconsciously.

You are gifted with great patience and determination and this can lead you either to the greatest successes through your life or to the greatest falls. What's really important for you is to have a sustainable life on all levels and you can actually achieve this through your life lessons of liberating yourself from material attachments. These material attachments also include other people and being attached to anything of substance, to your body, to someone else's physical body, to your looks, to things, to your clothes, to all things that you attach your emotions with too much. You need to be grounded, you need communication with nature, you want to feel secure and calm, you are a natural mystic. You are the provider, you are attuned to the rhythms of nature. You search for true values and you need constant approval of self-worthiness. You compete with yourself and always give yourself the toughest tasks and projects to work on, and this is one of the ways you build your self-confidence. You are capable of achieving amazing things in your life, you are often quiet and yet so powerful and determined, a realistic human being.

When it comes to meeting new people and letting them in your life, you take some time to see if you can trust them. Loyalty is extremely important to you; you can't stand betrayals and you can be very demanding because of that. You need to feel deep trust, you want peace and tranquility. Your energy is joyful and calm, you are patient and reliable, you choose the safe road. You are hardworking, you work toward building a solid foundation. You are responsible and you seek stability. You enjoy earthly and bodily pleasures, you honor touch and delicious food, you love feeling comfort and having comfort. You are the bringer of shapes and you shine the light of the spirit through the corporeal world. In order to become a true lover and fine artist of life that you are meant to be and bring abundance to your world and the world around you, your value system needs to change from time to time. You have to work on changing perspectives and becoming more flexible. You are an extrasensory being, you are a gardener of the earth.

Taurus using crystals can make wonders. As you are naturally connected with the cells of our planet Earth, communicating with crystal structures is profoundly meaningful for you. Crystals work with you too, they are very responsive, they make magic with your earth element and help you embrace and enliven all elements of existence from within. Working with crystals helps you refresh your strength when you feel immovable or stagnant. It will transform all your unconscious actions and patterns and turn them into something constructive and useful. It will enhance your vigor and all your qualities. It will transform your life and the way you imagine and manifest things. It will give you a completely different perception and taste of life. When you feel inert or lazy, crystals will bring that up on the surface and transform it. If you are stuck or blocked, or feel uncompromising or demanding, crystals can soothe, calm, and relax you and bring you feelings of safety. Your creativity and talents can be brought to light more easily while working with gemstones. It helps you become more of who you are through awakening your stability combined with freedom. It truly gets you in touch with manifesting universal codes.

Crystals which are the most influencing for you, dear Taurus, and that make you connected and plugged in with nature, stones which makes you free of attachments and in touch with the whole, are green jade, green aventurine, kyanite, amber, malachite, sapphire, emerald, rose quartz, lapis lazuli, turquoise, and tiger's eye.

The one crystal that corresponds with you in the best way and vibrates greatly with your field is green jade.

Green Jade

Green jade is not only perfect for bringing abundance and wealth to you, Taurus, but also for protection in different areas of life's mysteries. Its color affects you beautifully and reconnects you with nature even when you're away from it. This is your lucky stone, it harmonizes your being, it enhances grounding, it is your true guardian. It brings you great positive vibrations, it lifts your courage to go after your soul's desires. This gemstone supports your financial matters, it brings prosperity and feelings of security, but it also gives you vital energy and its usage provides natural growth without shocks, which is important for you since your nature loves stability and has trouble dealing with sudden changes. It protects you physically and emotionally, connecting the network between the body, mind, and soul.

This stone opens the doors of spirituality for you, which makes you more open to give and receive love that you deserve. It brings you back on your true path of faith if you wander off. Green jade protects you from getting lost in every way, be it physically or in your thought processes or with your emotions. It brings you back home. It brings you stability and strength to endure stormy periods, it charges you with joyful feelings. This crystal releases you from your inner doubts and clears the path so you can make healthy decisions and use your strength and deep emotions in the most valuable way. Jade gives you more freedom from

32

attachments, which ultimately makes you a true receiver of the treasures, always in sync with abundance which is all around.

Green jade also has fabulous powers to awaken your hidden talents and raise your potential. It is a powerful healing stone which brings you good luck. It balances your nerves and protects you from illness. It increases trustworthiness and fidelity, it helps you accept changes, it brings you peace and protects you from deceptions. It is also known as a dream stone. It protects you from bad dreams and helps in remembering the good ones. Through using green jade, you gain wisdom and remove everything that's in your way to receiving it, any negativity or wrong thoughts are being dispelled. It gives you tranquility and brings you back in touch with who you really are behind all labels and stickers that either you or those around you have attached to your personality.

Green Aventurine

Green aventurine is a calming stone and has a gentle nature. It gives clarity and better vision, and it provides deeper imagination. This crystal is strongly connected to Earth, and it transforms depression and anxiety into understanding and great hope. It distresses your body and mind. Its usage is extraordinarily good for any kind of growth, so it goes very well with your energy and nature, dear Taurus. It has a great effect in gardening, and it is beneficial for career advancement and prosperity. It keeps you calm and relaxed and releases you from inner pressures.

Green aventurine brings vitality, optimism, harmony, and comfort, it stimulates new things to come to you, it brings all kinds of renewals. It helps you with unresolved emotional issues and it heals your heart. It is also known as a stone of personal growth. It helps you move forward and break any frozen feelings, especially when you're faced with new and sudden situations or with any kind of change that you find hard to handle. It supports you in letting go of any unhealthy relationship and encourages a positive attitude towards life. It is an incredible healing stone and it helps you to navigate obstacles wisely and to achieve emotional calmness.

Kyanite

Kyanite is excellent for you, Taurus. It gives you power to speak freely and communicate more openly, to heal your throat chakra and release tensions from your voice. It is a high vibrational stone and it builds up your intuition and awareness, it helps you deal with troubling surroundings and to express yourself without any fear. It removes your overall resistance. It helps you create new connections. You receive confidence by its grounding and calming qualities, it opens portals for telepathic communication too. It gives you a calming effect through the body and provides great introspective abilities. It is a stone of connection and it is a perfect stone for meditation and attunement. It has an ancient connection with emotions and it deeply improves emotional connection between you and others. It has a healing and soothing influence if you're dealing with emotional or social anxiety attacks. It helps you reconnect with lost parts of yourself, it helps you to get back to previous emotions and memories in order to recover and rejuvenate those parts that were lost and forgotten. It has a grounding spiritual frequency and helps you mature on all levels. It can bring you healing dreams and help you understand things from your subconsciousness that you weren't even aware of.

Amber

Amber is actually a fossilized resin of ancient evergreen trees. It possesses old energy and wisdom of the earth, which makes it a perfect match for you. Amber connects you with primal energies of nature, bringing you power of the sun and Earth together. It can contain insects, seeds or leaves which were trapped in resin. It preserves them and carries their ancient evolutionary flow which brings ancient wisdom and knowledge. It is also used as a medicine, it is highly calming, it brings mental and emotional strength. It eliminates negative moods and it deflects negativity that's coming to you from others. It draws out and transforms negative energies.

Amber enhances self-healing, it helps you deal with depression and emotional healing, it is a highly protective stone. It brings revitalization and stimulates the body to heal itself, it holds ancient wisdom of Earth and matter within itself and it helps you with many physical diseases. It calms your mind and helps to remove physical pain. It has great connection with life-giving forces and it highly increases your creative self-expressive abilities. It helps you develop trust, peace, and wisdom. It is a mysterious stone with enormous purifying properties. It removes mental stress and brings you feelings of tenderness, safety, and individual strength.

Malachite

Malachite comes in different shades of green and it's traditionally connected to your sign. It helps you step out of your comfort zone and follow your dreams. It is a fertility stone, so it goes great with your natural potentials of growth and transformation. It frees you from limiting beliefs, it provides security, inner peace, and protection. It can detect danger and wake up your intuition to prevent possible accidents. Malachite is great for detoxing the emotional body, it releases emotional pain and cleanses you from traumas that may be stuck in your aura. It represents deep healing of Mother Earth and increases your ambition, it makes you more risk-taking, it helps you deal with many changes and challenges through life.

Malachite is a stone of transformation and it helps you accept changes more easily and become more flexible towards life and different situations that are happening to you. Malachite is a stone of manifestation and intention and it is incredibly powerful for metaphysical use. It is a deep energy cleaner; it draws out deep emotions to the surface so that they can be cleared and healed. It makes you aware of your own limitations and helps you liberate yourself from self-restricted patterns and programs.

Sapphire

Sapphire is another traditional stone of Taurus. It has many protective properties, and it is known as the stone of prosperity. It protects you from physical, emotional, mental, and even spiritual attacks. It enhances trust and faith. It preserves your honor and purity. It helps you express yourself freely without wearing any masks and reconnects you with your higher self, bringing you awakening.

Sapphire strengthens your motivation and brings sincerity in your work and actions. It brings you joy of enlightenment and magnifies your trust in yourself. It gives you more discipline and confidence in sharing your opinion and views. It is known as a stone of wisdom and it stimulates prophecy talents within you. It brings you deeper visions and helps you see the truth beyond the seen material realm, beneath physical appearances. It brings you calmness and feelings of order. It puts you in alignment with the Divine Source and universal force. It helps you manifest your desires.

Emerald

Emerald is considered to be a birthstone of Taurus, and it is also connected with Venus, your ruling planet, so it is great for love, beauty, and finances. It brings you feelings of universal love, compassion, and mercy. It encourages loyalty and patience which are your natural qualities. It also enhances creativity, improving your talents and artistic sides. It raises your feelings of self-worth and enriches your eloquence.

Emerald stabilizes and soothes, bringing you calmness and balance. Its green color stimulates your nature and is also great for attracting success in your life. It helps you remove blockages and wake up healthy responsibility towards your possessions in the material and emotional world. It inspires you to live in a more harmonious and generous way.

Rose Quartz

Rose quartz is another Taurus birthstone. It is known as the love stone; it resonates goddess energy, which is in sync with Taurus nature. It helps with fertility problems, it represents the Feminine principle, and it offers you deep spiritual love. It opens the heart and throat chakras. It increases self-love and unconditional love energies. It brings emotional health and reminds you to love yourself in order to love others truly.

Rose quartz helps you accept changes and go through them easily and lightheartedly. It teaches you compassion and helps you move on from painful events and emotions. It teaches you the true essence of love and it opens your heart on all levels. It helps you give and receive love more openly and free of fears. It will open your eyes in a way to recognize unhealthy relationships and encourage you to leave them behind. It purifies you from past attachments and past relationship issues. It heals wounds of abandonment, rejection, and loneliness, and teaches you forgiveness.

Lapis Lazuli

Lapis lazuli can energize your throat chakra and bring you into a heightened state of awareness. It also has protective nature and it empowers your thoughts, protecting you from physical and psychic dangers. It is a manifestation stone that helps you bring your ideas into matter. Lapis gives you mind clarity and helps you with making decisions. It provides great serenity and stillness to your mind, and it calms your senses and unlocks emotional blocks. It reveals your inner truth and puts you in touch with your personal and spiritual powers. It has a haunting beauty and it has been used since forever for protection, healing, and spiritual journeys.

Lapis lazuli offers gentle healing if you've been suffering from emotional trauma or any traumatic event. It brings and provides relief from emotional pain. It brings you deep insights and drags them up so you can acknowledge them, confront them, and process them. It enhances psychic abilities and stimulates your spiritual powers. It encourages you to take responsibility and be the one who is in charge of your life. It empowers your intuition and brings you emotional maturity. It improves your connections with others and makes you more compassionate towards them through your emotional growth.

Turquoise

Turquoise has many beneficial qualities for you. It attracts love, success, and money, but also protection, power, and luck. It is a purification stone; it clears bad thoughts and protects you from negative outside influences. It is used as a healing crystal, and its blue and green color gives an energetic flow between Heaven and Earth. Its vibrations are connected with life-giving elements of air and water which support your healing. It washes away any negative forces. It relaxes your mind and mental tensions and it heals emotional wounds.

Turquoise brings good luck and abundance, realigning your energy centers and connecting you with higher consciousness. It increases enthusiasm and brings out your hidden talents. It enhances your communication abilities and protects you from viruses, it provides physical protection. It protects you from pollution and electromagnetic smog. It is a strong and smooth stone at the same time that has been used by kings, shamans, and warriors across the world. It has an ability to merge your mind with the Universal source. It encourages you to accept yourself for who you are, to forgive yourself and others, and to let go of any regrets. It inspires you to honor and love yourself.

Tiger's Eye

Tiger's eye is excellent for grounding and stabilization. It improves your personal power. It gives you self-confidence and practicality, and helps you maintain calmness and creativity. It enhances your courage and integrity. This crystal was known as an all-seeing, all-knowing eye; therefore, it brings great vision and clarity. It provides great observation and divine vision. It is also linked with the third eye, stimulating your pineal gland and improving your ability to research the deepest parts of the soul.

It is also very connected to the physical realm because the tiger symbolizes material senses and supports you beautifully to become a master of your own body. It protects you from dark forces and curses, and it melts away all negativity as you work with it. It gives you motivation and brings success; it also helps you shift your perspectives and move easily through the changes. It is a powerful grounding stone and it brings you great focus and concentration. It brings you back down to Earth and makes you feel the present moment and be in it. It makes you feel your purpose here on Earth and remember what your mission is. It is especially useful for stubborn natures such as yours, as it brings openness and flexibility. It helps you let go of deep attachments and old habits.

New and Full Moon Rituals Using Green Jade

Green jade has multifunctional qualities, and it's especially useful during the moon phases. It connects the moon's emanating energy with the earth, and it charges the user with inner peace, calming the constant inner dialogue. It transcribes the moon's codes sent to Earth in the most healing ways. Meditating with green jade during the moon phases offers priceless opportunities for self-improvement. It helps you deal with energies that are hard to handle; it makes you more aware of your past and present. It can help you in many ways that you thought were impossible. Using this crystal under the new and full moon will meet you with your undiscovered talents, personalities, and ways of thinking and being. It can literally transform you and your life.

This stone is beautifully synced with the Taurus natural element of earth. Working with jade empowers your grounding and healing abilities, it is your sacred tool for abundance in physical and metaphysical spheres. It will make you more receptive of the divine energies and it will encourage you to research and discover your inner truth. It will make you feel gratitude and it reminds you of your deepest and most purposeful dreams.

Before the ritual, you can place it on earth and stand barefoot by the stone or sit in front of it. Feel its vibrations. You can also wear it while you sit under a tree. You should clean and charge your crystal before meditation and after it. You can cleanse it under water for several minutes, you can use your pure intention of purifying while doing it. You can run it through smoke, smudge it by lighting sage, palo santo, or incense and let this healing cloud of smoke cleanse it.

New Moon

The new moon ritual with green jade is an excellent time for you, Taurus, to initiate something new and invoke change in any field of your life. During this phase something new is born, and the crystal helps you attain your dreams and goals by removing your resistance to change. It breaks the limitations of the past and makes ideas and intentions available to be manifested in reality. On the new moon ritual, take your crystal with you, choose the way which makes you comfortable, you can go somewhere in nature, sitting or standing on the ground under a tree, or in your home because you already carry nature within, and so does the green jade. Place it in your lap if you're sitting or wear it near your skin. Your voice is so powerful, and you can sing or speak to your stone while focusing on your intention for the future. Feel the connection of your physical self with your mind and spirit through your voice as it manifests. Listen to your crystal because it starts communicating with you the same moment you start communicating with it.

You don't even have to speak or sing; you can do it by imagining you're doing it because the crystal hears that too. Your thoughts are calming down and you hear your intention more and more clearly. Imagine your intention being placed inside a light bulb and send it directly from your heart center to your sacred stone. Feel the crystal working its magic by unpacking it and sending it back to your center as a shining ball free from any firm shape. It is alive and spinning, it enters your heart chakra and spreads through the whole body, stretching outside of it and embracing you wholly and holy. It spreads from the center, and you feel vibrations through every cell from the top of your head to your toes. You become your intention.

If you feel any pulls from the past or attachments which possess you, send them to the crystal and release your emanation from it, hear the sound of your light and see yourself already there where your intention goes. It works as a magnet, you just follow without turning back. Your intention becomes visible and you sense it as if it is manifested right now. Continue releasing the past and just be in the now as long as you feel comfortable doing it. Your intention is sent, and your body and mind are cleaned from any distractions.

New Moon Taurus Affirmations

I accept and allow changes in my life
I nurture myself
I eat healthy food
I am abundant in every aspect of my life

41

I attract people who I can trust
I ground myself in order to rise
I am prosperous and successful in things which are good for me
I am safe
I have enough
I am resourceful
I attract… (whatever it is that you truly feel you need)
I am worthy of love, joy, comfort, grace, flexibility, and contentment

Full Moon

The full moon is the time to let that pain go, to break the attachments you hold from any traumatic or difficult situations from the past. It is time for you to accept the past and lessons and give them permission to leave. It is the best period for you, Taurus, to make peace with your possessions, to leave behind anything you feel is a burden, to release stubborn and fixed thought patterns, to get free from over-concerns, to get rid of the need for accumulation in order to feel safe.

It is of great value to work on transforming your value system, to enhance your strength and talents, and to let go of anything toxic for you. It is the perfect time to quit doing something that makes you unhealthy, to change your diet or daily habits, to change your state of mind, to send away repeated actions, to break the routine.

Your crystal helps you in many ways to accomplish all of this, especially during the full moon phase.

You can lie down and place your crystal on your forehead, or you can be in any position you like. Wear your crystal or hold it in your hand. Focus on your breathing and as you inhale, feel the body being filled up with conscious thoughts and refreshed ideas, feel your body as a night sky with the stars, or as a green field with soft flowers in bloom. Feel the whole of nature being inhaled, and as you exhale, release everything disturbing or burdening that's coming up. Feel the body being released from all the content, feel the emptying, feel the tension and attachments freely going away and leaving you. As you inhale again, you feel more of that freshness after each exhale since you cleaned and emptied it from the previous thoughts, beliefs, images, and anything that holds you back. Repeat this process as much as you feel the need to clean yourself from the past. Welcome the endings. Become your own master because you are the one, you just have to remember that and get free from what you learned to believe to be.

Full Moon Taurus Affirmations

I release and surrender all non-constructive patterns
I am connected with Mother Nature
I let go of what is not truly mine
I choose freedom over attachments
I cut the toxic ties
I use my common sense wisely
I am self-worthy
I love myself as I am right now, and I work toward self-betterment
through each moment
I take risks
I am powerful in who I am without any possessions
I support myself in a healthy and comfortable way
I allow my talents to unfold free of any fear
I have everything I need to live well and to prosper in all aspects of my
life

GEMINI

Gemini Sacred Stones and Rituals

Gemini is the first air sign and it symbolizes the twins. Unity from the source becomes duality and it searches for reunion. Being ruled by air, Gemini is connected with the lungs through breathing, and duality is demonstrated well through body parts that are ruled by Gemini: arms, hands, shoulders, lungs; there are two of each. Gemini also rules the nervous system and all these parts are sensitive spots for you. You can have breathing issues, anxious attacks, injuries including arms and hands. You are ruled by Mercury, the messenger of the gods and the trickster. You are the holder of the principle "I THINK." You bring the expressions of the mind and represent the split of consciousness into two hemispheres, the world of duality, separation between immortal and mortal. You are the bridge between the worlds, ruled by Mercury the Hermes who is the messenger and who moves quickly between the realms of gods, humans, and the dead.

Your minds run quickly and you are very intelligent. Being ruled by air, you are easy going and not so much into the material, you are primarily connected with the ethereal and the world of ideas, communicating those ideas and imaginations here in the material world. You give names to things you see, your curiosity is endless, you want to know everything and everyone, you share information so easily, you express your thoughts and emotions masterfully, you are a true storyteller, you transfer knowledge through every form of communication, you are the writer, speaker, actor, you show what you want with your moves, using your hands. You can adjust anywhere, easy as wind, you just run through any form. All these qualities within you can switch sides and turn into your weaknesses, into your extreme polarity. Your quickness in mind and body and your great curiosity can often put you in a lot of trouble. Being interested in literally everything you see, hear, feel, smell or touch, you can become lost in many roles which catch your attention. You want to taste everything and share that experience, you move on to the next role while you still play the first one.

Because of this, your mind works 24/7, becoming restless instead of restful. You can't focus on one thing or two things, your attention goes in so many directions. You are not just the twins and duality, you juggle with many personalities, often you do it well, but this is something that eventually brings you nowhere and makes you unsteady and unreliable. You can also get yourself in trouble when you talk about something when it is not the right moment for it; your talkative nature can create damage when you spontaneously share something that you later discover you shouldn't have shared. Your childlike innocence needs to mature so that you can give birth to your true soul's mission. It doesn't mean you'll lose your childish nature and youthful appearance, it means you'll become the master of your spoken words and of sharing words of truth and wisdom in truly amazing ways, brightening and inspiring the minds of others, bringing new thought patterns into existence. You need something to calm and distinguish your thoughts in a healthy way so that you know which thoughts to follow and which to dispel. If you fall into gossiping, you should work to transform it into lively intellectual conversations. You are a beautiful entertainer, you can learn anything, and you can offer easy and unconventional teachings to others through fun and creative expressions.

Your versatile nature can bring you chaos if you don't know how to handle it. Your hyperactivity can be used constructively instead of letting it ruin your nervous system. You are a free spirited, open minded, and eloquent being. You should strive towards equilibrium of spirit and matter. You hold the potential to reunite split forces, you are enormously skilled to use words as magic and synthesize separated realms. Your Gemini qualities are holding keys to the process of an alchemical wedding, the sacred marriage of the feminine and masculine principle, bringing the inner male and inner female archetypes together in a constructively working flow, the awakening of the human. You are also one of the human signs in the Zodiac; you bring together the left and right hemispheres of the brain, you bridge and join two pillars into sacred union with an unshakeable base, you connect and merge masculine and feminine principles, giving birth to the full potential of the divine spark into the physical world of substantial expression.

Crystals are important, helpful, and supportive for you, dear Gemini. You should work with stones throughout your life to learn the secrets of meditation and to have clear communication with the world of spirits. You gain tremendous abilities when you connect with your gems. Your mind becomes your sacred tool and you stop being a slave to your thoughts and curiosity. Through communication with crystals, you can achieve and realize your core and essential role in this life. It becomes easier for you to witness the whole process of your mind and to have master control over it without taking advantage of it. You become the witness of your personality which gives you the possibility to change and modify any aspect of your expressions. Crystals reconnect you with your intuition, which tells you what's good for you and others and what is not. The point is to discover how to properly use your qualities and not to get rid of them. Crystals have the power to join you with your true abilities and make you aware of what you are capable of, to reconnect you with your path to unity with source energy.

Crystals that have codes which are connected with you, Gemini, which are helpful and make you come to equilibrium states more easily, are agate, chrysocolla, apophyllite, howlite, chrysoprase, serpentine, celestite, pearl, tanzanite, and rutilated quartz.

The one crystal which is the most beneficial for you, dear Gemini, which makes you achieve and unlock your skills and potentials, is agate.

Agate

Agate is your sun crystal; it is connected with Mercury, your ruling planet, and it brings out your possibilities in the best way possible. You have a very dynamic personality and it helps you deal with your unfocused attention. It gives you an ability to remain concentrated when you feel confused or disoriented. It stimulates honest communication, it calms your active mind, it supports you to keep your attention on what's important instead of running from one thought to another. It makes speaking easier and removes tactless and unconscious talking. It provides clarity, helps you with keeping secrets, and it makes you develop maturity, trust, and inner stability. Using this crystal helps you overcome your tendency to talk too much about things that drain your energy, it stabilizes you and gives you strength to become centralized between polarities. It stimulates precision in thinking and communicating, it draws you back down to Earth when you fly too high and feel lost in the air, it is your grounding crystal. It connects you with gentle vibrations when you feel nervous or anxious. If you feel mentally unstable, this stone will bring you a peaceful state of mind, it will clear away your thinking process, it makes you quiet. Agate recovers your mind and body when you feel exhausted, it helps you deal with stress and situations when you easily get bored.

This is a stone of relaxation, cleaning, and balancing yin and yang, which are very important for you, since you are ruled by duality and are often pulled between two extremes. It offers you great ability to meditate and reveal your hidden talents and skills through it. It brings you vitality and frees you from pain. Agate is a multilayered stone, so it fits perfectly with you because of your multilayered personality and interests. It helps you become aware of what is actually really working for you and what you can let go of without feeling stressed that you're going to miss some experience, chance, or opportunity. It has a healing effect for lungs and blood vessels, it returns you to a calm state if you feel that you're going crazy or when you're too distracted. This crystal also gives great protection from negativity, its power encourages introspection and contemplation, it provides you with confidence in spirituality, it brings equilibrium between your thoughts and emotions, which are usually distorted. This stone sends you soothing vibrations which have a therapeutic influence on you, it clears your way towards becoming the purest version of yourself, it makes you use your voice with honesty and truth, it reconnects you with your soul and helps you see yourself authentically, it brings you closer to your true emotions and makes you love yourself as a whole being. Love all the twins you carry within.

Chrysocolla

Chrysocolla calms mental tensions, it brings peace and patience, it improves communication and encourages you to share knowledge clearly and truthfully with others so that everyone can bear fruits. It is known as a stone of teaching, so it goes very well with your nature. It brings benefits to artists, writers, teachers, speakers, and actors, which are all your potential talents. It also calms emotional stress. It offers inner strength and stability. This crystal is good for nervous disorders and for lung issues. It brings protection from psychological damage and clears the blocks that may prevent you from gaining wisdom.

Apophyllite

Apophyllite is a pyramidal shape crystal often called the "meditation pyramid." It expands your mind and enhances spiritual growth. It's connected with the crown chakra and opens up connection with higher realms. It energizes your soul with lightness and keeps you relaxed, it enables deep insights and visions which are connected with some current situation in your life. It attunes you to truth. This crystal is extremely powerful for meditation and it helps you release negative thought patterns. It offers new wisdom and new perspectives. It helps you deal and resolve emotional traumas from your childhood and bring back your natural lightness.

Howlite

Howlite teaches you patience and strengthens your memory. It helps with issues caused by an overactive mind. It is a calming stone which stimulates calm communication and helps with insomnia problems. This crystal boosts your desire for knowledge and constructively channels a flood of energy. It stills your mind and removes nervousness and rage; it calms turbulent emotions and absorbs tensions and anger that's pointed towards you either by you or those around you. It assists you in reaching your goals and inspires you with new ideas. It helps you let go of distracting thoughts, and its cleansing vibrations have a soothing effect on your mind and body.

Chrysoprase

Chrysoprase helps soothe an overactive nervous system. It's a powerful balancing stone, it brings compassion, deep healing, and love for the truth. It brings Universal energy into material existence. It stimulates creativity and brings out hidden talents. It increases grace and equilibrium, it helps you balance your conscious mind with your unconscious mind, it reduces selfishness and carelessness. It cools off intense emotions and removes anxiety and depression, it heals your inner child and promotes a neutral state of mind, it supports your love for yourself and ensures healing of the heart.

Serpentine

Serpentine recovers your mental and emotional disturbances, it detoxifies the blood and the body, and it creates a protective and energetic shield around you. It helps you gain more control of your life. It enhances clearing of all chakras and it especially stimulates the crown chakra which encourages opening of psychic abilities. It corrects your imbalances, it aligns your field with the earth, and it calms you down. It helps you regain wisdom and memory from past lives, it transforms poisons and negativity, it balances your mood swings and enhances your spiritual rebirth. Serpentine is a soothing crystal which helps you repair your emotional body. It is also a stone of independence and encourages you to become truer to yourself and others.

Celestite

Celestite is a powerful healing crystal. It has high vibrational qualities, and it is a soothing and uplifting stone. It opens and calms your mind and brings mental clarity. It helps you get in touch with divine beings and opens up access to the spiritual and psychic world, it reconnects you with your guides. It encourages you to step into spirituality and bring positive forces into your life. It promotes harmony, inner peace, confidence, love, and gratitude. It increases feelings of calmness and serenity; it calms mental chaos and sharpens your mind, and it supports you emotionally and cleanses your etheric body. This stone assists you in maintaining balance and leads you toward enlightenment.

51

Pearl

Pearl symbolizes and brings purity, wisdom, self-acceptance, innocence, and personal integrity. It brings you deeper understanding through experiences, it helps you learn the lessons and gives you inner confidence, and it balances your aura and protects you from chaotic feelings and thoughts. It supports and strengthens the growth of pure love. It brings you truth, sincerity, and chastity; it enhances your loyalty and elevates your spirit. This crystal keeps you relaxed and protected. It helps you release accumulated emotional pain and it clears your heart and mind. It absorbs negative energy and helps you deal with the truth of self. It teaches you to find the purpose of your essential nature.

Tanzanite

Tanzanite helps you slow down and take it easy. It establishes a connection between your mind and higher realms. It is linked with the heart chakra, third eye chakra, and throat chakra, and this connection opens up a whole new perspective and point of view for you. It supports your concentration and beautifully opens up your communication abilities, it helps you communicate from your heart. It has a very balancing effect for highly active people which benefits you enormously, dear Gemini. It corrects extremes in your personality, it makes you more trusting and centered within yourself. It supports release from old patterns and karma and activates your spiritual growth. It promotes a strong sense of self-control and brings you optimism and inspiration, it gives you a sense of direction, it connects you with the power of the divine mind.

Rutilated Quartz

Rutilated quartz brings physical and mental balance and stability. It is also "the illuminator" of all the chakras in the body and connects your entire being. It helps you with decision making and it cleanses and energizes you. It encourages you to go to the root of the problem, it helps you to go deep within and gain clarity on the duality of your mind, it is your psychic antenna, it promotes self-realization and finding inner truth. It stimulates divine imagination and an expanded state of consciousness. It helps you with healing emotional wounds, it brings you better understanding of yourself and others. It protects you from lies, phobias, anxieties, and psychic attacks. It reminds you to keep your feet on the ground and your sight up to Heaven.

New and Full Moon Rituals Using Agate

Agate crystal is extremely potent during the new and full moon phases. You should use it during these cycles in your rituals and meditations to enhance centering and grounding your energy.

Agate absorbs the information through the light of the moon and filters it and purifies it for your well-being. It works according to your intentions and vibrations, and according to your emanation it transforms the forces of the moon for your self-betterment. Using agate during moon cycles can make wonders and bring incredibly deep root changes into your life. It can transform your life and infuse it with new codes of your being. It will make you more focused through your life, more ready to face challenges and accept changes, more willing to move on and feel life in its essence, feel the nature of your own being. Your conscious intentions and inner work with crystals and the moon's energies will reshape your reality and perception. You will gain access to various dimensions of your mind and awareness.

Before your meditations and rituals with agate, you should cleanse it and energize it. You can use the light of the waxing moon to charge it before using it, but you can also bury it in the ground over night or energize it while holding it in your hands. You can use reiki, conscious breathing into your crystal, smudging it with the smoke of strong and healing plants like a palo santo stick or any other incense you love using. You can cleanse it with water or with sound-tuning healing frequencies. Feel free to experiment and find your favorite way. Don't expose it too much to heat.

New Moon

During the new moon, day or night, you should be concentrated on your future goals and things you want to accomplish, your new self, your image of where you want to be. It is time for planting new seeds, visualizing whatever it is you wish to manifest. It is an excellent time for using your crystal and communicating with the Universe and your inner guidance so that you can bring forth what yet needs to be born. Before the ritual, you can write down a list of the things you wish to see manifested. Concentrate on each intention while you're writing it down, make a list of the things you wish to learn and things that make your life easier and more loving.

You can wear your stone on your skin or hold it in your hands while you focus on your intention. Close your eyes, feel and hear the complete silence surrounding you, listen to this silence, become the silence. Imagine you're so light that you move through the air being carried by the wind. If you have trouble feeling this, you may start by imagining that there's a shining rope above you connected with your head which lifts you up gently.

Visualize your intention as reality, go into that image and paint it as you want it to be, make your intention alive by imagining it being manifested, travel within your mind through these images. You have that power, your crystal will help you to keep your vision alive. Feel your body light as a feather, floating freely and entering into the picture of the future you wish yourself to be in. If your mind loses focus, don't worry. Send those distractions to your crystal, point them directly to your stone and it will absorb it and dispel the distractions. Go back into the state of silence, listen to its wisdom. Reconnect with the source, imagine the reality you wish yourself to be in. Imagine one whole day of that new reality and live it through your meditation.

You can write down your experience after you're done with this practice. Write down how you felt while you lived there, write down your distractions, your fears, your observations. Write down emotions you went through, small details that caught your attention, struggles you had to overcome to keep your intention clear, write down when you felt good, when you felt down, when you felt free, when you felt blocked. You can also send these thoughts to your crystal and write it down mentally using your crystal as your journal.

New Moon Gemini Affirmations

I trust that all will unfold perfectly
I am patient and I trust in the process
I communicate clearly and truthfully
I restore and hydrate my energy
I am still and my thoughts are constructive
I am always learning
I think for myself
I honor the power of my words
I attract what is the best for me
My curiosity brings me the information I need
I know everything is possible
I am flexible and adjustable without losing my authenticity

Full Moon

This phase of the moon has enormous power to release your tensions and mind chatter, to get rid of toxic emotions, thoughts, attachments, people, jobs, routines, and whatever it is that you feel is a burden or an obstacle.

Wear your crystal on your skin while you sit in any position you find comfortable. Or, place it on your body where you feel you need it if you decide to be in a horizontal position.

Focus on your breathing. Feel the air you inhale and how it fills your lungs, feel your whole body rising as you inhale, feel the air coming out while you exhale, feel the whole rhythm of the inhale exhale cycle, the rise and fall of your lungs and belly. Focus on the beat of your breathing and just be. Allow the crystal and the full moon to purify your mind and body. Feel how you're being charged with etheric light energy. Your electromagnetic field around you starts glowing and you feel the vibrations through and around your body. Try to maintain these feelings free of any thoughts and desires; just focus on your breath. Do this as long as you feel comfortable.

When you finish, stay in the same position for a couple of moments and feel your body and mind relaxed and clear, refreshed and recharged, free of any thoughts and emotions, just the pure feeling of being. After this you can also write down your impressions and speak them to your crystal, with your mind or words. It is your confidence stone, you can speak without any feelings of fear, you can speak your truth and be honest, there's no one to judge you. Your spirit understands everything you're going through and your crystal connects you directly with it.

Full Moon Gemini Affirmations

I have the power to change what's not good for me
I respect my ideas
I attract love and abundance

I choose to speak honestly and bring knowledge and wisdom to others
I am open to infinite possibilities
I let go easily
I have multiple skills and talents and teach others how to use them
I express my thoughts and feelings with trust and purity
I embrace the troubles and turbulences that come my way
and gain wisdom through it
I allow the Universe to guide me
I accept my current situation and let it teach me valuable lessons
I allow myself to become my best version

CANCER

Cancer sacred stones and rituals

Cancer belongs to the element of water. It's the first of the three water signs, ruled by the moon which represents eternal change through cycles, high and low tides. Cancer rules the chest, breasts, stomach and womb—everything connected with growth and nutrition. As a Cancer you are concerned with emotional security, you carry embedded codes of Divine Mother archetype, the healer, the child. You are connected with birth and life-giving properties, the beginning of summer. You carry the "I FEEL" principle within and represent the incarnation of the souls into the human body; that's why you're associated with home, motherhood, carrying, giving life, breast feeding, nurturing, etc. You are sensitive and changeable; your activities are based on feelings, and being under the guidance of the moon, you are often under the spell of fluctuations of moods. You can be restless and hyper-emotional, which makes you feel insecure and anxious, then you seek for security and safety of home and tend to become attached to your protective shell in order to isolate yourself from being hurt. This is not something bad. You have an instinctual protective nature which keeps you safe, but when the threat is gone, sometimes it's hard for you to believe it's safe to come out, and you may still stay inside and strongly hold on to the past.

Your inner child needs to mature and experience the outside world in order to grow and become the radiant source of love. It doesn't mean you have to destroy your shell—no, it is your natural protection and you need it, but you have to learn when to use it, not to abuse it. It has a great purpose. You need your own place of tranquility from time to time to rest and retreat. You highly feel emotions and states of people around you and it is natural to separate occasionally from the atmosphere you've been exposed to so you can recharge yourself and come out when your batteries are full. Your perception is intuitive and you're inward looking, you possess huge inner strength, you need time to withdraw, to process your emotional experiences and then to reemerge into the world. You are deeply connected with roots and tradition, you are protective, healing, nurturing, food- and family-oriented, domestic, you have exquisite qualities with everything that has to do with caring. You are empathic and intuitive, comfort-oriented, but you can also be too worried because of your need to protect others and yourself. You can easily become dependent and insecure, shy and attached to the past.

You belong to the most active sign of the water signs. You need action and change and you have emotional intelligence, which helps you to sense any trouble before it appears. Your intuition is high, you're also very receptive and because of that you can take in so much emotions and feelings from different sources, which eventually become sedimented. Holding it inside is harmful for your physical, emotional, and mental health, so you should find some kind of outlet for this. Crying is a great alchemical process which clears out and empties accumulated states, it can reset you and purify you from toxins, taking you back to the zero state from where you can freshly start again, washed over by a feeling of relief.

You need a loyal and supportive group of people who become your family. You are sentimental and if you're far from your roots and home and your tribe, feelings of homesickness quickly start embracing you. You possess enormous constructive and destructive possibilities. You are creative in many aspects of life and romantic and dreamy qualities run through you; you need to learn how to surf through these waters so you can become a true master and healer, to become your own parent without the need for outside protection. You hold the keys to your awakening, you have the power to become an outpouring source of light.

Using crystals has such a powerful influence for self-betterment and self-healing. Crystals are deeply connected with water, and water itself is a kind of fluid crystal. For you, Cancer, stones have extremely regenerative powers, they immensely help you revitalize and restore your energy and your bodies: physical, emotional, and mental. They recharge you and renew you. They are supportive when you're feeling insecure or drained. Gemstones are healers as you are, and you can use them as protection too. When you feel betrayed or hurt, crystals assist you in feeling better, detoxifying you from habitual emotions and past traumas. Crystals help you in dealing with immaturity, and they offer you easy access to the Source and reconnection with your inner healing abilities. They remind you of your true emotions, distinguishing what is yours from what belongs to others. Crystals encourage you to become who you're meant to be.

Crystals which are in resonance with you, which are in the same vibration with your nature and spirit, which are the most beneficial to you, dear Cancer, are red jasper, moonstone, opal, rhodonite, emerald, calcite, selenite, beryl, rainbow obsidian, and chalcedony.

The one crystal which is truly responsive to you and in correspondence with your wishes and life goals is red jasper.

Red Jasper

Red jasper is known as a supreme nurturer stone, which is very beneficial for you, dear Cancer. It offers steadiness and emotional sustenance, it stabilizes your connection with nature, and it is very useful for gaining emotional stability and maturity. It motivates you beautifully and regenerates your mental and emotional body. This stone solidifies your roots which are very important to you; it is a highly nurturing and grounding stone. It is also known as the rain bringer and the stone of wisdom and courage. It stimulates health and builds spiritual awareness too. It creates a strong and powerful energetic flow within you and helps you release inner wounds with understanding and forgiveness. It calms your emotional body and helps in healing your scars.

With your conscious intention it can make you achieve balance and acceptance of life's circumstances. It supports you in dealing with struggles and revitalizes you after life's battles. This gemstone brings you determination and focus, it offers growth for what you already have inside as a seed. It recharges your energetic and emotional field when you're dealing with any kind of weakness, it offers vitality when you're feeling down or unwilling to make a move. It helps you move forward when you'd rather move backwards like a crab; walking backwards is sometimes necessary, but you have a natural tendency to continue in that direction when that path is done, and working with red jasper helps you reorient and focus on attaining your goals and constructively using what you've accomplished during that process of traveling through the past.

Red jasper helps you face unpleasant situations and tasks. It encourages you to continue working towards your goals and to complete what you started. When there's no one around to give you a hand and support you, this stone builds your inner strength to turn inward and become your best friend and advisor. This gem helps you strengthen your aura. It activates your base chakra and stimulates the rise of energy; it assists you greatly in manifesting creative ideas. It is extremely powerful during meditation and contemplation, it eliminates negativity, clears your emotional anxiety, helps you see and feel your emotions in essential ways, makes you recognize the true purpose and value of what you're going through and why you feel the way you do.

Red Jasper makes you more aware of lessons you're learning through your emotional center, bringing you self-mastery by grounding, protecting, and nourishing your core. It's a stone of empowerment, it helps you overcome feelings of being hurt and violated, it protects you from domination of others, it's great for building and rebuilding self-confidence. It encourages you to deal with feelings of shame or guilt, to easier release emotional and subconscious burdens you carry. It makes you lighter and helps you maintain stability. It offers insights on family issues and unresolved past traumas. This stone is your friend and it protects you; it brings you in alignment with your true powers and mission through this life. It reconnects you with your basic needs and offers self-security. Its comforting essence eases you and makes you see the true colors of your deep attachments; it helps you let go of what's no longer needed so you can continue growing in a natural way towards your center.

Moonstone

Moonstone is your Zodiac stone. It teaches you natural rhythms of existence. It helps you unlock what's hidden deep beneath your surface. Iit takes you on an inward journey and helps you dive into depths of your being and bring the forgotten and missing parts to the light. It brings out the best in you, it supports and stimulates your heart and mind, it promotes clarity and inner vision. It helps you recognize emotional patterns. It eases sadness and changes. This crystal stimulates your visions and strengthens your intuition and introspection. As its name says, it is strongly connected with the moon, which is your ruler. It reconnects you with your roots and subconscious material and helps you overcome childhood memories and attachments.

Opal

Opal is an emotional stone that inspires love, hope, innocence, and purity. It protects you from easily absorbing other people's feelings and thoughts which you absorb naturally. It's a stone of loyalty and faithfulness, it clears the emotional body and boosts your will to live. It has high water content within, so it's supremely supportive for you, it helps you in shifting emotions constructively. It encourages freedom and independence. It helps in dealing with buried emotions, releasing anger, and expressing your true self. Opal assists you in seeing destructive emotions and supports the process of letting them go.

Rhodonite

Rhodonite is your emotional healer. It calms the nervous system and brings you back to the center. It helps you heal emotional wounds and scars from the past, it provides nurturing of the inner self. It's known as a salvation stone; it relaxes and harmonizes you and improves self-esteem. It promotes the energy of love, it orients you toward generosity, and offers greater satisfaction to you. It calms emotional shocks and feelings of panic; it gently frees you from self-destructive tendencies. It balances your emotional body and promotes forgiveness; it activates the heart chakra and helps you remove the feelings you don't need anymore. This crystal encourages true friendship and love of others. It's a stone of compassion and it is your emotional balancer.

Emerald

Emerald is your traditional birthstone. It brings you stability and peace. It's a stone of great vision and intuition that promotes friendship, domestic bliss, loyalty—it's the stone of the heart. It's great for self-healing and it has a calming effect on your emotions. It clears away feelings of victimization and encourages you in dealing with the misfortunes of life. It strengthens your physical and emotional heart centers, it helps you understand your own needs and emotions, it enhances unconditional love and unity. It makes you see more clearly where you're out of balance and what you resist, it helps you see what's controlling you. It assists you in understanding others in a detached way, it encourages you to live and act from the heart.

Calcite

Calcite is a powerful cleanser of energy that brings joy, wholeheartedness, and love. It removes stagnant energy, it heals and energizes your physical, emotional, and mental states. It's a powerful remedy, it is a spiritual stone, it helps you realize that spiritual realms are not so separate from your everyday life. It connects emotions and intellect, it stimulates insights. It helps you interpret your dreams and transform negative emotions by understanding their true meaning. It calms your mind and teaches you discernment, it charges your emotional intelligence and helps you become more energetic. It teaches you that the past and future are contained in the present.

Selenite

Selenite is your direct link to the spirit. It's an abundant stone, it promotes purity and makes you be honest with yourself. It can be used to access past and future lives; it clears confusion and helps you see the bigger and deeper picture of your existence. It protects you from negative external influences, it inspires profound peace, its high frequency enhances opening and clearing of the crown chakra. It encourages your desire for inner transformation and helps you accept the changes and challenges that you're facing. It reconnects you with your highest purpose and makes you work for the highest good; it is a protective stone that wards off toxic energy and protects you from letting others drain you emotionally.

Beryl

Beryl is very beneficial for you, Cancer. It helps you let go of unwanted emotional baggage, it supports you in going through the process of emotional healing. Beryl encourages you in dealing with constant stress. It has a balancing effect on your nervous system; it recharges you after a long time of healing and recovering. It cures laziness and keeps away negative and destructive thoughts. It has a detoxifying effect and it increases your courage, confidence, and sincerity. It promotes happiness and marital love.

This crystal reminds you of your talents and helps you find the answers you're looking for. It unlocks your potential and unleashes your inner strength. It helps you to learn how to relax and prevents you from being overstimulated, it removes distractions and makes you more adjustable to changing circumstances. It is your tranquilizer for heart and mind, it reawakens your love for yourself and those around you.

Rainbow Obsidian

Rainbow obsidian has strong protective properties. It helps you discover and reveal the root cause of emotional traumas and supports you in letting go of the past, to leave behind whatever it is that's limiting you from moving forward. It helps you to learn and work through your emotions, supports you in rewriting your life story, and helps you release attachments that are left in your heart. It replaces negative thoughts with empowering ones, it offers you soft-heartedness, gentleness, and sensitivity. It encourages you to focus on the good; it guides you to the right direction when you're feeling lost and don't know where you're going. It brings hope and energy into the blocked areas of your emotional body. This crystal absorbs negative energy from your aura and supports you in processing your pain and stress. As its name says, it reminds you that there is a rainbow waiting for you after the storm, and it encourages you to not give up and to keep an optimistic view on life.

Chalcedony

Chalcedony is a powerful healer because it is a nurturing stone and really goes well with your nature, dear Cancer. It gives you strength to make positive changes in your life and it removes sadness, self-doubt, and unwanted feelings. It helps you rebuild your confidence and strengthens your self-love. It promotes brotherhood and enhances group stability, it absorbs and transforms negative energy and bad dreams, it brings you feelings of harmony and balance between your mind, body, emotions, and spirit.

It's a stone of peace and peacemaking. It brings you stillness, calmness, and stability. It promotes emotional balance, vitality, endurance, friendliness, and kindness. Chalcedony increases your emotional honesty and inspires you to speak from your heart, to express your emotions with generosity. It improves your self-perception, it boosts your creativity, it motivates you to become a better person and helps you get rid of toxic emotional involvements. It enhances optimism and feelings of joy. It reconnects you with the best parts of yourself.

New and Full Moon Rituals Including Red Jasper

Working with red jasper during the moon phases is very supportive and benevolent. Its master healer role comes into fruition under the new and full moon periods. For you, dear Cancer, it has a very motivational and healing effect. Using this crystal during the moon cycles helps you gain stability and balance, it grounds you and calms you, supporting you to heal emotional overload and any feelings of stress and anxiety.

Red jasper is amazingly helpful and useful for meditations and attunement with the moon's energies, and during long-term use it transforms your mind, body, and soul. It will transmute your inner state of thinking and feeling, it will make you appreciate life and see it in a completely different way than ever before. This crystal under your conscious efforts and work will reconnect you with Source, it will reconnect you with the divine and Mother Nature; it will give you a new vision of everything around you and within you.

Before using it you can charge it under the full moon moonlight by holding it between your hands. You can also put it under running water for a couple of minutes to enhance its abilities, and water is your ruling element, so you can boost some extra power with water and crystals together. You can also clean it by smudging it, passing the stone through the smoke and setting your intention for cleansing.

New Moon

The new moon time gives you full potential to use your crystal and your intention to make something new, to send your wish to the cosmic waters and speak with your emotions in a renewed sense. It is a great time to give birth to something new, to get ready for a fresh start. You can focus on self-healing, on getting things done. You can focus on your love life and evoke your inner guides and emotional intelligence to support you in manifesting your heart's intention.

You can wear your crystal near your chest or hold it in your hands. If you can, be somewhere near the water: lake, river, sea, ocean. It helps you stay calm and feel nature, but if you're not in the position to do this, don't worry. You can do it with your mind; close your eyes and travel to the place you imagine to be the most comforting and inspiring for you. Explore that place and allow yourself to fully feel it and observe it.

Breathe and listen to your heartbeat, feel how it's connected to everything around you, focus on your intention and connect it with your crystal, become aware of its presence. Feel those new vibes coming to you, imagine you're under a waterfall being washed with crystal clear water, set an intention and feel the drops of the water pouring on you with new ideas and visions. Let it revitalize you, allow your crystal to receive your message clearly, feel yourself recharged through every splash of the waterfall, feel your crystal as a part of you, feel the transfer of the energy and love. Let the water and its lively movement enliven your body and heal your emotions, let it remove obstacles that stand in the way of making your dreams come true.

Your crystal gives you a green light to accept this new energy coming your way, it allows you to accept the water's blessings and feel the soft ground under your feet which supports you. Water and Earth together create new life and electricity, feel it through your body, let it do the work for you, you just have to be and let it do its magic. Feel free to plant the seed of your intention into the ground and see how it's being engulfed and surrounded by water. Let it grow and see it manifested. Feel the grace and joy of being alive, be in this state as long as you feel comfortable and slowly open your eyes when you're done.

New Moon Cancer Affirmations

I trust myself
I accept and honor my protective instincts and I use them wisely
I accept the future without letting the past interfere
I choose to love myself without feelings of guilt
I value my intuition and listen to its quiet wisdom
I cherish my feelings and let them exist without judging
I choose self-acceptance
I bring my dreams into manifestation
I am healthy in body, mind, and soul
I take the best care of myself
I am always home when I'm connected within

69

Full Moon

The full moon phase is special for you. Since the moon is your ruling planet, it has a deep effect on your soul and emotions, your past memories and things you hold inside, your family and love life, your faith and destiny, your childhood and relationship with your parents, your life path and attachments you carry. This is a supremely potent time for you to empty out what's no longer needed, to free yourself from unwanted and destructive thoughts, emotions, memories, pains, images, people, food, habits, etc. This is your time to create new karma, to rewrite your life script. Using red jasper crystal helps you to go through this more easily and less painfully.

Hold your crystal any way that feels enjoyable, take a position that makes you feel good, close your eyes, focus on your inhale and exhale, forget about everything else, only breathing exists. When you feel there's nothing left but breathing, imagine yourself being your parents and a child at the same time, there's no one but you in the whole existence. This crystal supports you to get in touch with your inner parents and child. Allow them to coexist, feel them as a part of you and feel yourself as a part of them.

While you're doing this, feel less and less identified with those roles, just accept them for who they are, love them and respect them for everything they've done or haven't done, understand the highs and lows of life, see the lessons you had to go through, get insights on how growing up created the whole pattern for your future life, how it affects your present relationships, your love life, your career, your talents, your unfulfilled wishes, your partners, your friends, your emotional life, your pains and joys… You can shift between roles of mother, father, and child; speak with each other from everyone's angle, listen to the child, let the child know that you care for him/her, let the child know that you love him/her, ask for forgiveness, feel the light of being forgiven and giving forgiveness to others. Hear what all of them have to say to each other.

Let the crystal take away all negative emotions and thoughts and words that you still feel. Cry if you feel like crying, let your voice be heard, let your heart heal and transform the buried emotions into feelings of mercy and understanding. Understand that it was all part of the process for you to grow up and become who you are today, allow yourself to change for the better and forgive whatever is left to be forgiven. Feel the easiness of letting go, feel the joy of not interfering anymore into the past dramas, unlock your true potential, unlock your inner wisdom through cleaning your past, and feel your emotional intelligence rising and leading you towards a greater destiny.

Full Moon Cancer Affirmations

I am connected with the Divine Mother
I am safe and protected
I am brave and strong; I can do it all
My home is my heart
I welcome healing love into my being
I accept the pain I had to go through
I embrace my strengths and weaknesses
I am not to be deceived
I choose healthy relationships
I honor the power of my emotions
I live in the present and find safety within myself

LEO

Leo Sacred Stones and Rituals

Leo is ruled by the sun and fire. Leo the roaring Lion—born as a king, "the king of the jungle," promotes "I WILL" and "I SHINE" principles, rules the heart, spine, spinal column, and upper back, and these body parts are strong and problematic at the same time. Leo is that highest point of space, culmination of the summer when the sun is in its highest position shining brightest, it is the illumination, coming to light, rising of consciousness, self-actualization, and all things Self. All these beautiful golden properties make you confident, optimistic, generous, majestic, and strong. You have a protective and forgiving nature; your enthusiasm inspires many, and your ambition will encourage others not to give up. You carry principles of creativity, playfulness, and expression; your inner sun brings warmth and joy of being alive.

The sun represents the self and it gives you a strong sense of personality and ego; that's why it's easy to become trapped in personal identification, to become too proud of yourself, self-centered and egotistic. You can become too self-involved and demanding which brings you down and makes you lose your true powers. You have a tendency to dramatize things and get involved in dramas quickly; this is not bad as long as you are aware of the situation and know how to deal with it. You can use your talents to entertain yourself and others, you are a natural performer, you shine as a star, you naturally attract the public and people admire you for who you are, but if you're focused only on your appearance and can't get enough of being admired and honored, if you always need praise from others, you easily become narcissistic and arrogant, feeling like you deserve everything for free, like others are there to serve you and applaud you. You have to become conscious of these things because they steal your sunshine, they weaken you and make others see you as someone who is always showing off and looking for attention.

Your inner sun needs to be in balance with your sense of purpose and meaning. You are born to bring light to others, to shine, to emanate the truth from yourself, from the center of your heart, from the heart of the sun—from the core of Leone. You are a courageous, magnetic, highly social being with strong personal integrity. Your stability is beautiful and your intentions are pure, you have a big, kind heart and you deeply care for others' safety. You are direct and others most often respect you for that, your honesty and loyalty makes others feel safe in your company. You have to take care not to become addicted to being adored and feeling like you're above others. You are here to share and spread the light, you are a solar fire, a symbol of individualization, you have to become aware of your actions and work, to gain mastery over your lower nature. You possess life-giving energy, a charismatic and radiant personality, and your purpose is to develop your higher self and become compassionate towards others. Then you can really enjoy the center of the stage wherever you are.

Using crystals can help you and motivate you to pour sunshine from within and absorb the information through the sun, to keep your vitality and level of energy high, to purify and electrify your being on physical, mental, and spiritual levels. Working with gemstones will support your generosity and enhance your stability. It helps you realize your power and understand your personality from a higher point of view, and it inspires your brave heart. These sacred stones will support you in dealing with your ego, getting you closer to its advantages and disadvantages so you can learn the whole mechanism and understand how to use it in the most constructive way. It helps you meet your heart's desires and teaches you how to implement and integrate your natural qualities and talents. If you fall into delusions of grandeur it can help you see it for what it is, to understand the meaning of different levels of consciousness and reasonably experience the path of falling and rising through direct personal challenges.

You are naturally gifted with beautiful potentials and your conscious effort in using crystals can reconnect you with your light and make you more aware of many different possibilities you are capable of. When the stone is energized by your intention, it can work as a natural reminder for you, it helps you recognize your unconscious instincts and gives you the ability to transform them into self-knowledge; it helps you through the processes of peeling dysfunctional layers in order to gain sovereignty over your life. Crystals remind you that you have a crown and that having a kingdom demands great responsibility and wisdom, that you are a noble King/Queen who brings light and forgiveness, that you are a carrier of fire who awakens true passions in every heart.

The best crystals for your growth and healthy development of the seeds you carry, the stones which are the best supporters for you and which make you self-righteous, are black onyx, pyrite, peridot, sunstone, rhodochrosite, golden topaz, labradorite, and chrysoberyl.

The one crystal which is the most beneficial to you and which synchronizes you with your heart and passions is black onyx.

Black Onyx

Black onyx is your birthstone. It keeps your mind free and makes you flexible, it gives you effective control of your strength and prevents draining of your personal energy. It is a grounding and protective stone; it has incredible power under your pure intentions. It helps you to find confidence and control over your physical, emotional, and spiritual body, it brings balance and integration of duality. This stone helps you to choose positive actions, it brings stamina, firmness, durability, self-control, permanence, and constancy. It transforms aggression into inner strength, it supports your ability to endure and persist ups and downs through all kinds of life challenges. It makes you feel at ease with yourself and others, it helps you release painful memories and cleanse the heart and base chakras, it opens channels for happiness and good fortune. It is said that this stone stores a lot of old memories and when used properly it has a power to set your soul free from karmic cycles and repetitions, it clears blockages and makes space for your true essence to shine. This crystal helps you heal from feelings of grief and sorrow, it supports your stability and provides grounding when you feel overwhelmed by extreme and excessive passion. It enhances your vitality and boosts your immune system. It has great healing properties.

It helps you pick back up energy, it turns weakness into strength, it protects you from negativity and psychic harms. It provides a strong connection with the earth while allowing you to aim high for guidance. Onyx helps you connect with your subconsciousness and communicate with your higher self. It cools your hot temper when needed, it brings you closer to understanding your purpose here on this planet in this life, it helps you clear bad karma. This crystal helps you to clearly see your virtues and vices and become aware of their presence within you. It supports you in the process of self-correction and self-betterment, and it helps you deal with difficult people and situations. It provides greater focus on what's important and supports you in letting go of what no longer serves you. It brings you back to your core, it reminds you of your true nature, it helps you get rid of stress and troubles and reconnects you with the heart center. This stone will enhance your power to become the true carrier of the sun and bringer of light, to share justice and generosity, and understand your role in this incarnation, to radiate your warmth and become your own best friend and assistant.

Pyrite

Pyrite is connected with the sun, which is your ruling planet, and it has a great effect on you, Leo. It is also connected with the earth and the fire elements; its name contains the word "pyr" which means fire, and its golden yellow color attracts wealth and prosperity. It's a stone of intellect and protection too, and it's also a mirror crystal that reflects truth and reality, it enhances focus, creativity, desire for action, and mental stability. It gives you a new way of thinking. It is known as the "stone which strikes fire." It encourages you to get rid of anything old, it protects you from energy leaks, it dispels fear and self-doubt, it enhances your self-growth and makes you recognize your potential.

Peridot

Peridot is one of your birthstones. It helps you bring back light into your life. It is a healing stone and brings harmony and peace, it has magical powers and protects you from nightmares, it provides great emotional healing. It is also connected with the sun and gold, it increases self-esteem and promotes happiness, confidence, prosperity, positivity, and abundance. It's a great source of high frequency vibrations, it lifts your emotional state and brings feelings of joy. It's excellent for spiritual work too, it protects you from psychic attacks. It enhances self-assurance and supports you in achieving your dreams. It gives you the ability to step back from unnecessary drama, it helps in healing when the ego is hurt, and encourages self-growth and realization of your true nature.

Sunstone

Sunstone has a strong connection with the sun, and it's also one of your birthstones. It increases your willingness to help others and boosts your generosity, strength, and personal power. It reflects the qualities of light and brings honesty, clarity, and compassion. It reconnects you with the source of light, warmth, and life. It brings comfort and nurturance, it makes you take better care of yourself and others, it lifts your spirit when you're low on energy or depressed. It promotes leadership qualities which are your natural potentials, it helps you see the beauty around you and align with your higher power and wisdom. It gives you a sense of abundance and appreciation, it brings inspiration, and helps you with emotional dependency.

Rhodochrosite

Rhodochrosite is a stone of the heart chakra that helps you embrace your personal power and brings love into your life—self-love, love of others, spiritual love, universal love, and unconditional love. It brings deep emotional healing and supports you in feeling worthy. It supports the opening of your heart and attracts your soul mate. It eases depression and sadness, it transforms painful memories, and awakens the inner child by bringing feelings of joy, innocence, and happiness. It is also supremely beneficial in healing past romantic wounds and deep pain; it is a remedy of the soul. It also helps in learning and connects you with your higher mind. It encourages you to make necessary changes in your life. It allows you to accept and forgive yourself and deal with traumatic experiences more easily.

Golden Topaz

Golden topaz is a crystal of truth and forgiveness that soothes, heals, regenerates, stimulates, and recharges you. It helps you manifest your desires, it brings true friendship, romance, a life partner. It's a bringer of good luck and fortune. It brings abundance, peace, and joy. It helps in finding your true purpose and destiny. This crystal strengthens your focus and helps to discover lies and deception, it removes damaging thought patterns, it helps you activate cosmic awareness, it has a strong connection to the Divine. Golden topaz makes you more aware of your emotions, thoughts, and actions. It promotes concentration and it releases you from tension. It helps you deal with depression. It increases well-being and health, it stimulates self-confidence, and helps you achieve your goals and perfection.

Labradorite

Labradorite is known as a magical stone. It eliminates negative energy and reconnects you with intuition and subconsciousness. It shows you the way to the truth, it is the dreamer's stone, it brings self-awareness of inner spirit, it provides great protection, it unlocks telepathic abilities and prophecy. It detoxifies the body from drug abuse, alcohol, and tobacco. It brings full attention; it's connected with the third eye and crown chakras, and it helps you connect with your higher self. It prevents the loss of energy. It tempers excessive ego and arrogance. It brings out the best in you and helps you enter deeper states of consciousness. It brings the truth to the surface and expands your understanding. It brings calmness and eliminates painful memories.

Chrysoberyl

Chrysoberyl gives you peace of mind, mental clarity, and self-confidence, and it strengthens your will for self-healing. It is great for discipline and gaining self-control. It keeps you safe from accidents and transforms negative energy into positive and uplifting vibrations. It charges you with the truth and self-mastery and improves your ability to gain wisdom and self-knowledge. It increases your personal power and sense of generosity and compassion. It helps you improve tolerance and create harmony. It promotes peace and forgiveness. This stone also brings abundance and wealth in material and spiritual worlds, it boosts your confidence and pride in a healthy way.

New and Full Moon Rituals Using Black Onyx

The energy and usage of black onyx crystal is especially heightened during the new and full moon periods, when your conscious work with the stone increases the intention and allows the cosmic forces and love light to connect with you directly.

This gemstone works in your favor when you meditate with it during the moon cycles. Using it consciously and intentionally during moon cycles can increase your capacities and potentials. It will work in your favor and it will dissipate unwanted energy. Meditating with this crystal will transform your life, your habits, and your lifestyle. You will feel motivated and inspired to shift yourself for the better. It is wonderful for meditation and for alignment with the cosmic forces and rhythm. Black onyx has a powerful influence on you under the new and full moon meditations and rituals; it will make you aware of many things you couldn't notice before, things about your life, your past and your present that you couldn't see in any other way, it will open your eyes to new worlds and possibilities. It will make you aware of your weaknesses and strengths and will inspire you to work on them and heal them. It will improve and upgrade your qualities and transform your deficiencies.

You should cleanse your crystal before using it. You can cleanse and charge it in many ways. You can use a smudge stick and place your crystal in the stream of smoke, you can charge it under the full moon light and leave it for a whole night outside, or put it on your window under the moonlight. You can also put it in the sunlight for a couple of hours or wash it in seawater or a river. You can even use rain if it's raining outside. Choose your own way and enjoy the exchange of energies.

New Moon

The new moon's energy is about creating and manifesting. It's time to plant seeds for the future and set your intention in a new direction, to use your creative talents and visualize what you want to embody and give birth to. Using black onyx is perfect for you, dear Leo, because it will help you keep your intention pure and focused during your sacred ritual. It makes you more open and receptive to step into your clean state and make a true wish that makes your whole existence more lighthearted.

You can hold your crystal in your hand or between both hands, or you can place it somewhere where you feel you need it the most. You should be somewhere peaceful where nothing can disturb your concentration and peace of mind. You can either sit or stand, choose whatever position you find the most joyful for you. Be quiet with yourself, focus on your heartbeat while you breathe, make sure you do this for a while until you feel you entered your inner field. Visualize your inner sun as a glittering spark rising from your heart, feel its warmth and vibrations, feel it growing and glowing, feel how it spreads shiny golden rays, feel its emanation from your core, feel how it expands through your whole body while the initial spark stays in the center. Feel the comfort of brightness hugging you from the inside. Now spread it even more, feel and visualize how it expands more and more. Feel how it embraces your whole body, and feel how it spreads outside and protects your body from within and without. Hold that feeling and vision, just stay in that feeling of yellowish golden rays coming in and out continuously. As you become one with your heart center and your sun, you become the warmth and rays and the center, your crystal absorbs and resends new energy of love light to you. Send your intention through the rays to the sun and to the crystal, see your wishes fulfilled, manifest your vision through that light, send it to your crystal. Your intention is stored and memorized, the new moon cycle and the stone's power will continue the process of making your wish come true. You can continue feeling enjoyment of the energies and vibrating rays splashing in and out as a fountain, revitalizing your mental, emotional, and spiritual bodies. Meditate until you radiate.

New Moon Leo Affirmations

I love and honor every part of my being
I value my passion for expression
I shine from within and bring warmth and joy
I honor my personality and my unique talents
I am self-aware and self-confident
I create what I intend
I choose love light instead of power over others
I allow myself to feel what I feel
I recognize the true power of my heart center and allow it to guide me
I bring courage and inspiration into lives

Full Moon

You should take your time during this phase of the moon to work on cleaning and pouring out whatever has been held for too long, what holds no purpose anymore, what has expired and what doesn't contribute to your present and future self. Do the inner work and research from within, find what's no longer serving your highest self. Find what disturbs you and what makes you anxious, bring it to light and let it transform.

You can go somewhere out in the sun or in some place of yours to speak with your higher self. Take your crystal with you and hold it or wear it. Do as you like, dear Leo—it listens to you just by being close to you. Close your eyes and connect with the perpetual fire that shines freely and lightly, surrender your past wounds and troubles to its purifying magic, let it burn those emotions and thoughts which hold no value anymore. Your crystal removes the blockages while you concentrate on the cleaning process. Self-healing engines are on and you feel revitalized over and over again through every breath you take. Imagine the pure essence of light and feel how it purifies and detoxifies you as you breathe in and feel filled with love light. While you breathe out, imagine you breathe out the fire which burns what's left to be cleaned. Keep breathing and repeat this process of transmutation of light into fire and fire into light, feel how they both serve you, feel the wisdom of their sacred work and feel the weight falling away from you, feel how fire and light take away heaviness from you and pour you with renewed and refreshed energy. During this process you are freed from ego, you just are. Remember your true essence, you have the power now to remember that you are the child of the sun. After this, return to your personality as a new you. Step into ego mode more naturally and maturely, one step closer to self-realization.

Full Moon Leo Affirmations

I am free to be who I am
I let go of what hurts me
I allow myself to shine
I respect my heart's desires
I speak my truth
I connect with those who support my true essence
I attract true love based on purity and sincerity
I listen to my intuition instead of defensive thoughts

83

I use my fiery energy to spread love
I choose conscious actions

VIRGO

Virgo Sacred Stones and Rituals

Virgo is all about practicality, usefulness, efficiency, service, grounding, inspection and perfection, alchemy, and cycles of nature. Virgo is a virgin, a maiden, ruled by earth element and the planet Mercury, often connected with Chiron and Ceres through healing and nurturing aspects. Virgo rules the digestive system, stomach, abdomen, spleen, and gut; that's why you have a strong feeling in your gut. Your high intuition comes from this connection with your gut instincts. You hold the power of sorting wheat from the chaff and you're extremely good with details. Your analytical and sober mind is always scanning, analyzing, and sorting. Your intellect is brilliant; you are born with instinctual understanding of nature and its wisdom. You have natural healing powers working through you. You are health-conscious and you take perfect care of everything. You honor purity and cleanliness, and you are well organized and independent. You possess rational thoughts. You hold the "I ANALYZE" and "I SERVE" principles, but you are not a servant. This aspect should be understood in a higher and deeper way. Your service is divine and you embody cosmic principles, serving them to mankind. You represent consciousness grounded into the body. You're connected with the grain goddess, and when it comes to service, for you, it actually means healing and teaching humankind—teaching about growth, growing your own food and plants, gardening, and teaching natural science like mathematics, biology, and astronomy.

Your health-focused mind and detail-oriented thoughts can make you become obsessed with your daily routines and habits, how you spend your time, and how you organize your schedule. You can become nervous and anxious if you notice something going out of your control. Your nervous system can be endangered when you fall into these freak-out zones. You have a tendency to disassemble everything to its smallest parts until it becomes meaningless and loses its essence. This can drive you crazy. You have to remind yourself of the meaning behind the matter, behind the endless deconstruction of images and the whole. You are prone to perfection, which can lead you toward self-criticism and criticism in general. You can become hard to please and unable to get any satisfaction. Your mind can cause you a lot of troubles and pains; you can become too cautious, which can block your natural potentials for teaching and healing. Your shaman powers become hidden and you can fall into never-ending analysis of things, emotions, people, events, and life. You have a tendency to become a hypochondriac if you allow your mind to take full control of you. You can also become obsessed with work; you can become a workaholic and forget the other aspects of life. All these troubles, which can become your reality, are not as bad as they seem. These are all hidden golden potentials. Your need for perfection can take you to the greatest achievements; your hard work becomes sacred when it's done through love instead of being used as an escape tool. Your focus on health can become healing and helpful for many in many ways. Your analytical mind can solve a lot of problems and find the most practical solutions.

You are selfless, stable, honest, precise, intelligent, and service-oriented. You should watch out not to become a servant and serve others just for the sake of serving. You are much more than that. You have a sacred mission to merge microscopic parts into a whole, to alchemize earthly and cosmic energies, to synthesize and incorporate various parts, to become whole and see the perfection in everything around you. You show others the science of diffusion and fusion; you show constructive expression of wholeness and all of its parts.

Crystals are powerful transmitters and receivers which help you develop your powers and potentials. These gemstones provide direct communication between micro and macro worlds and connection with your inner guides. They work as natural chargers and energizers. Stones also absorb unwanted and disturbing energies around you as well as those within you. Crystals help you clear your mind and calm down. Your overthinking tendencies can be reduced, and you can release critical thoughts more easily when working intentionally with stones. Together with your intention and energy, crystals work for your benefit and get you into a relaxed state of mind and body. Your natural grounding abilities will increase, and you'll feel supported when facing your inner blockages in order to get rid of various conditionings.

Crystals can improve your life and make you live more truthfully. They can also help you soothe your mind and get a better perspective on your personality and interactions. The crystals that can help you do these things are moss agate, amazonite, azurite, fluorite, blue tourmaline, petrified wood, zircon, and blue topaz.

The one crystal which is amazing for your usage and has the best improvement qualities for your nature and potentials is moss agate.

Moss Agate

Moss agate is known as a "Gardener's Stone" and it fits perfectly with your aura and inner energies. It helps you connect with nature and brings you calmness. It absorbs your anxiousness and nervousness, transforming them into stabilizing and strengthening qualities. This stone brings emotional and energetic balance. You become able to harmonize all disconnected parts and receive a clearer perspective so you can act from the place of knowing. It brings grounding energies and reconnects you with your heart chakra.

This gemstone recharges your electromagnetic field; it recovers your state of mind and body, it brings back meaning to your life. It helps you find the meaning of life and situations that you're dealing with. Working with this crystal will help you recover from a busy lifestyle and overthinking; it will help you clear the mess you're going through and get yourself in good and healthy shape. It will make you feel more energized and willing to take better care of yourself without over-worrying or fixating on obsessive thoughts. It will make you feel lighter and more easygoing if you overload yourself with hard work. It releases you from pressures by bringing you back to a zero point. It brings you more confidence by helping you get rid of daily stress. This crystal will free you from unnecessary over-analyzing, and it will prevent any possible panic attacks. It makes you more accepting of the things you can't control. It will reduce your need to control everything around you; it will refocus your mind when you feel you're excessively going into details.

Moss agate reminds you that you're the master of your life and that you're the only one who creates trouble for yourself. This makes you aware that you have the power to transform everything that distracts you from living life as you truly should. It promotes growth and supports your work. This stone brings abundance and wealth, it is incredible for healing, it brings back hope, and helps you reconstruct your life and habits in the most beneficial way. It brings prosperity and reconnects you with Earth. It creates magic if you're planting something; it supports the health of plants and reminds you of the importance of self-care. It draws expansion and stimulates you to spend time in nature, to recharge your body and communicate with the spirits of nature. It improves and awakens your skills; it activates your will.

This crystal brings you better focus and more awareness of the things around you, and it sharpens your perception and makes you become a more conscious observer. It reduces pain and provides wondrous recovery from periods of illness. It recovers you after feeling low and helps you strengthen your body. It increases your concentration and sets you free from conditioned feelings and thoughts. It is supportive in any kind of therapy and helps you get in touch with your soul's purpose. It helps you find beauty and inspiration in life. This is a stone of strength and it reconnects you with Mother Earth. It helps with your metabolism and detoxifies your body. It supports recovery of the whole immune system. It helps you express your emotions and tear down those walls of protection you carry around while still keeping you safe and providing healthy protection.

Amazonite

Amazonite is your calming friend. It's a soothing, earthy stone which helps you get rid of tensions, fears, self-doubt, and worries. If you've experienced emotional trauma, this crystal provides you great healing. It's an empowering stone because it brings you emotional courage, strength, harmony, and balance. It brings peace, truth, and constructive self-love. It calms your brain and nervous system. This gemstone empowers self-discovery and self-awareness. It's an encouraging stone that increases your self-esteem, self-confidence, and compassion; it improves communication. Its name is connected with warrior women known as Amazons and connects you with that kind of bravery and courage. It reconnects you with your heart and throat chakras, and it helps you manifest your dreams. Amazonite helps you clear your mind and release accumulated negative energy. It supports your talents and connects practicality with intuition. It empowers you strongly if you've been disappointed or self-destructive.

Azurite

Azurite has a rich, deep blue color. Its high vibrations resonate with the third eye chakra, and it develops psychic abilities. It was used as a guiding stone toward enlightenment and was known as a "Stone of Heaven." It is believed to open celestial gates. This crystal helps you clear your mind and remove any negative patterns, to get rid of outdated beliefs and cloudy thoughts. It recovers your brain activities. It brings your mind back in balance if you've been exposed to overthinking and over-worrying. It stimulates your intellect; it grounds your energy and physical body. It releases your subconscious material of emotionally charged thoughts, and it helps you recover your mental state.

Azurite enhances your intuition and helps you make the best decisions. It greatly resonates with your sign and helps you improve your talents and transform negative patterns which prevent blooming of your potentials. It has powerful healing energy. It helps you keep your body strong; it releases you from confusion. It enhances wisdom and maturity, and it helps you restore balance and control.

Fluorite

Fluorite has an enormous range of colors and is known as the most colorful mineral in the world. It's a beautiful and luminous stone and is also known as a "Genius Stone." It supports free flow of life energy and activates all chakras. It supports both brain hemispheres to work together in balance. It brings near perfection; it increases brain activity and recharges your will for learning. It allows you to focus on what's important; it removes distractions from your thoughts and brings them into cohesion. It helps you let go of the small details which distract your focus and concentration. This crystal stabilizes your system and helps you transform chaos into healthy self-organization. It empowers your spiritual powers and charges your aura. It helps you absorb new information and ideas; it improves your creativity and makes you more inspired and explorative.

Blue Tourmaline

Blue tourmaline has powerful protective and healing energies. It comes in many shades of blue and promotes happiness and inspiration. It boosts your passion and self-confidence and is known as the best supporting stone for you, Virgo. It brings you greater understanding of yourself and others. It enhances compassion and tolerance while balancing masculine and feminine energies in the body.

This crystal is very powerful for getting free from paranoia and panic because it brings serenity and flexibility. It activates your throat chakra, which empowers your communication abilities. It brings you courage and self-esteem to speak in public and express your thoughts through your voice so that others can understand you. It activates your subconscious powers and connects you with your true feelings. Tourmaline empowers you to express yourself freely without feeling threatened by your surroundings, and it helps you release things that you keep locked inside. It brings powerful intuitive insights and increases self-respect. It's excellent for meditation, and it helps you coordinate between physical and metaphysical worlds. It promotes emotional healing and release from your emotional bonds.

Petrified Wood

Petrified wood is also known as fossilized wood. This is a stone of roots and ancient knowledge. It calms you and grounds you if you're feeling fear, anxiety, or panic. It brings you patience, consistency, and steadiness. It calms your nerves and brings you feelings of stability and security. It's a transformational stone; it helps you go through periods of changes easily, and it gives you a sense of peace, making you aware of what's important and what's not. It encourages you to accept situations you cannot control and let them go instead of getting stressed and obsessed about them. It helps you establish deep roots and reconnect with your ancestors and past lives. It holds ancient magic and wisdom and shares it with you. It makes you aware of your grounding powers and foundations, and it recharges your faith and helps you become more trusting in the process and obstacles on your road. It helps you overcome any turbulent states and periods. It makes you capable of transforming past struggles into inner strength.

Zircon

Zircon has great spiritual and physical healing properties. It helps you overcome feelings of loss; it brings courage, protection, happiness, and self-confidence. It brings you spiritual energies and wisdom and allows you to transfer them down to the earth. Zircon increases your integrity and dignity, and it recharges you with self-worth feelings. It releases you from shy feelings and encourages you to express your inner states. It helps you to act efficiently and be more organized; it inspires you to connect with your spirit and express it through matter. It provides guidance when you need it and removes depression, anxiety, and grief. It helps you overcome jealousy and possessiveness. It brings you into alignment and helps you let go of anything old. It awakens your virtues and helps you get out of difficult situations, and it enables your growth and maturing.

Blue Topaz

Blue topaz supports self-expression and the spoken word. It stimulates your throat chakra and third eye chakra. It helps you understand complex concepts and ideas, and it enhances healthy self-control, openness, and honesty. It encourages you to speak your own truth and stimulates good communication. It improves your creativity and increases attention. It supports you in achieving perfection in a constructive way while bringing peace to your life. It boosts your intuition and helps you reveal secrets. It brings truth and wisdom. It recharges your body and brings healing and soothing energies.

This crystal enhances forgiveness and helps you let go of having to be right all the time. It brings abundance, generosity, and good health. It makes you more receptive to love and affection. It's excellent for metaphysical work and meditation, and it assists you in attuning to spiritual healing and inner guidance. It helps you find solutions to your problems and encourages you to bring hidden emotions to the surface.

New and Full Moon Rituals Using Moss Agate

Moss agate is perfect to use during the moon phases because it is a great attractor, absorber, and transformer. It will boost your intention. It's beautiful to work with this gemstone through meditation because it will help you get into the meditative state if you generally experience distractions while meditating.

Moss agate is connected with the spirit of earth, which is your ruling element, and it benefits you strongly during the new and full moons. It brings new beginnings that resonate with the new moon, and it provides releases of all kinds, which are ultra-powerful during the full moon. Moss agate is amazing for meditation, and it will make you stabler through long-term usage. It has the power to relax you easily and get you into meditation with a feeling of flow and relaxation.

Rituals and meditations with crystals are very powerful tools for self-development and self-improvement because they work a link with spiritual realms and subtle energies that are all around you and within you. It will raise your consciousness on all levels of your existence, and will transform your life in a big way if you use it with pure intention. It will make you discover and rediscover your hidden talents and gifts. It will perfectly ground you and garden you.

You can cleanse and charge moss agate in many ways. You can put it under the light of the full moon, or you can place it somewhere near a window or out in the open to leave it overnight to charge. You can use saltwater to cleanse it. You can also smudge it with sage, palo santo, burning cedar, pine, or lavender; you can also just place it somewhere near greenery. Use your intuition to tell you which way is the best for you.

New Moon

During the new moon phase, you should focus on your intention. Work with your crystal and interact with it; the crystal is already connected with you, so you just need to set the intention and bring yourself into a state of calmness. The new moon is perfect for new beginnings and initiations of all kinds. Your intention plays the main role, and your stone is a magical bridge between you and your intention. It makes it possible for you to cross obstacles and meet your goal. It helps you reach your desired destination.

Wear your crystal near your skin or hold it in your hands. If you can, go somewhere where you can be in touch with the earth and nature, but it's completely fine if you do it in your own private space where you can be yourself and away from any kind of disturbances. Make yourself feel comfortable. Play some calming music if that helps you relax. Set your intention and feel it coming out of your chest; feel it as an energetic ball radiating purity and new life. Follow it, go with it, travel out of your body together with it, let it take you for a ride through time and space and beyond, and fly with it. Let it show you all the beauty and challenges on the path that leads to its manifestation. Cross that bridge and enjoy the ride; see the landscapes from the left and from the right side of this bridge. Take a look to the sky and feel your feet. Embrace all the sides of the image. Tune into a 360-degree view, feeling all the seasons at once and letting the magic of your intention work. Follow the navigation and just set yourself free. Experience all the possibilities of achieving your goal, and turn off your thinking—just feel the feeling and watch with your inner sight. Any fear you feel, any worry, no matter how small that fear or worry is, your crystal will absorb it and it will encourage you to continue walking and experiencing. You can gain great wisdom through this inner bridge crossing. Do this as much as you are feeling it and experiencing it. When you finish, feel how the energetic ball of your intention enters through your chest transformed, free from blockages that crystal sensed through you, free from fears that are cleared and healed.

You can use your journal to write down your experience. You can write about the troubles and pleasures you felt on your road. This can help you see where you're blocking yourself through various fears, but also where and when you're feeling good, as well as what makes you be at peace with yourself.

New Moon Virgo Affirmations

I am strong and self-reliant
I graciously accept my talents
I understand and accept myself as I am
I understand and accept others as they are
I make wise and self-caring choices that support my life
I shape my future in a balanced dance
I trust my intuition and perception
I join separate parts into a purposeful whole
I am a magical healer
I have all that I need

Full Moon

The full moon's power is extremely strong. It can make you feel more emotional than usual, and you can get into feelings which are hard to handle; therefore, meditation and work with crystals during this phase are very advisable. It's an ideal time to ground yourself during this cycle and use it to clean your space, inner and outer. It's a significant period for releases of all kinds, for liberation from toxic patterns, for letting go of outdated labels and thoughts.

Wear your crystal near your skin and take a position which suits you the most. You could be sitting or lying in a comfortable position. Make sure there's nothing that disturbs your peace, and close your eyes. Focus on your breathing, both the inhale and exhale. Feel your whole body and relax any areas where you feel tension. Tune into your breathing. When you feel you're tuned in, imagine yourself becoming a tree, and feel its roots reaching deep in the ground. Use your imagination to draw the whole image—the surrounding of the tree, day or night, which season it is. Sense every cell of it. Feel you're anchored deep in the earth; feel how strong and stable you are. Sense the branches growing and rising, feel the leaves, feel the breeze, and listen to the sound of dancing leaves. Feel the whole tree. You are the tree—the roots, the trunk, the branches, and the leaves. Imagine and feel every part of it.

As you inhale, feel the energies from the core of the earth rising and coming to the surface of the ground through your roots. Continue lifting the energy all the way to the top and feel it through the whole tree. As you exhale, feel the energy coming out of the leaves and send everything you want to get rid of out into the open, letting the waters from above clean your energy. Now, when you inhale after this step, feel the transformed new energies from above spirally entering through leaves and moving downward through the branches reaching the roots. When you exhale, refresh the core of your being by sending transmuted energy deep down through your roots. Your crystal helps you stay focused, and it transmits these energies through this transformational process. Continue this process as long as you feel comfortable and as long as there's material for transforming and letting go. This opposite direction flows while you inhale and exhale through the tree and allows you to feel the whole organism of existence and see how it creates and transforms life and death.

Full Moon Virgo Affirmations

I allow my inner guidance to transform me
I let go of striving for perfection, and I accept the world as it is
I let go of self-criticism and self-control
I accept life as it is
I express myself freely and share my knowledge with others
I see divine work in service to others and I serve with joy
I choose to develop my potentials
I know where and how to invest my energy and time
in the best possible way
I allow myself to rest knowing that the world
won't stop without my help
I release all my illusions and painful memories
I am already where I'm supposed to be,
and I accept and honor my journey

LIBRA

Libra Sacred Stones and Rituals

Libra is the sign of balance and relationships, symbolized by scales. It represents divine justice and peace. It is the second air sign and is ruled by Venus. Body parts connected with Libra are the kidneys, lower back, endocrine system, and skin. Kidneys maintain the balance of fluids in our bodies, and balance is of key importance to all of you born under the sign of scales. You should take care of these body parts; they are either very good and healthy or they can cause you issues.

You were born with the need for harmony. You strive for public and personal harmony as well as for equilibrium between consciousness and unconsciousness. You are a peacemaker and artist and a lover and diplomat. You are an equalizer of two opposite sides. Your affirmation is "I BALANCE," and this is your ultimate goal—to achieve perfect partnerships, relationships, marriage, and social life. You seek to bring true communication, cooperation, and compromise in companionships. You can be seen as someone who avoids conflicts and direct confrontations; you can become disturbed and anxious when others wait for your decision and action. You are not someone who uses force, and you want to have all sides satisfied. You see everyone's angle and point of view, and others often misunderstand you because you have an objective mind. You can step away from personal judgment and objectively see the whole situation. You have the power to be a righteous judge, but you can experience difficulties if you insist on avoiding conflicts. Sometimes you have to go through it and learn through it. When you're unbalanced you can become passive-aggressive, self-indulgent, indecisive, and defensive, and you can go into hedonism and become manipulative and dependent.

You want to achieve idealism in all aspects of life. This can cause you troubles on the path, but you have a strong and high mental potential; your intelligence is high, and this makes you aware that troubles and hard times are your guides. When you recognize your own unbalanced sides, your own masculine and feminine, left and right sides of the brain, conscious and unconscious drives, inner and outer, then the true awakening of your soul begins. When you let go of a strong desire to maintain peace at all costs, you will develop true mastery over unbalanced energies and prevent unnecessary draining. You have talent to make things beautiful, to give artistic eyes to others, to create high-level relationships, to awaken emotional intelligence between you and the other. You learn through mirrors and projections with others. You gain understanding of the self through the reflection of others.

You have refined perception and codes for beauty and proportion written within you. You want meaningful relationships. You are friendly and fair-minded, you love life, and you want to enjoy it with others. You have exceptional understanding, and your intuition tells you exactly how others will react and what they need. You have a natural talent to make friends with those who seem to be enemies. You have the power to turn every situation into your favor; you are charming and polite, and your kind nature can change the whole atmosphere for the better.

You have the potential to awaken from this material dream to realize that spirit and matter are working together all the time, that neither spirit nor matter is ever in dominion, but that they are in perfect balance all the time. You can gain wisdom of intuitive weighing, knowing what to keep and what to throw away, what's valuable and what's worthless. Your sign is represented by a blindfolded woman. This means inner sight, intuitive vision, knowledge, true divine justice, the righteous one, virtuous, high-minded, and moral in the true essence.

Using crystals can get you closer to becoming the true you, the real you. Gemstones can connect you with your ethereal being by making you more present and inspired for true knowledge and higher meaning. Working with crystals can transform you for the better. They give you a greater understanding of the world around you and within you. These highly vibrational minerals are incredibly beneficial for healing and personal and spiritual advancement. They will support you in achieving balance, as they are natural balancers and will work wonders with your energy and natural abilities. You can completely transform your lifestyle and habits while working with them. They emanate and absorb by giving you what you need and taking from you what you don't need. You can become more aligned in every way. When used correctly and from the heart, their power becomes limitless and miracles happen. They help you bring your relationships and family matters into order; they open communication with your emotional center and give you the ability to express yourself to others without fear.

The crystals which are the best for you, which resonate with your frequency and help you bring balance and peace, bring understanding and knowledge, bring wisdom and true connection with yourself and others, are ametrine, morganite, blue sapphire, lapis lazuli, opal, clear quartz, blue lace agate, black tourmaline, and chiastolite.

The one crystal which helps you the most and which is also your birthstone is ametrine.

Ametrine

Ametrine is your birthstone. It's a combination of citrine and amethyst quartz, so it makes a perfect match for you. It connects and balances physical and spiritual realms. It embodies citrine and amethyst energies by amplifying the energy of both stones and enhancing universal equilibrium. It holds the duality of male and female energies within itself; citrine and amethyst have opposite characteristics, but in ametrine, they are linked harmoniously; their strength and power are merged beautifully. Ametrine is filled with life and wisdom. It promotes the ultimate state of perfection, balancing male and female principles and qualities. It stimulates creativity and learning, and it keeps you inspired and focused. This crystal rejuvenates partnerships and long-term marriages; it helps you keep relations refreshed and renewed, bringing new vital energies to everything that's been stuck or unable to move. It brings together physical and psychic worlds, helping you to achieve balance in everything that you do. It provides creative and original solutions to problematic situations. It helps you make wise decisions and it quiets down your inner discussions that prevent you from making a wise choice. Ametrine supports your meditative state. It strengthens your concentration and enables spiritual and intellectual emulsion. It connects your solar plexus chakra and crown chakra, and it stabilizes you and brings harmony with others, which is very important to you. Ametrine gives you mental and spiritual clarity. It brings unity of opposites, providing deeper and higher understanding of interaction between you and others, past and future, now and then. It helps you see the processes unfolding from above and from below, and this gives you knowledge of how and why things are happening in a certain way. It promotes cooperation, peace, and tranquility. It protects you from negativity and psychic attacks; it releases you from emotional, physical, and mental blockages.

This crystal empowers your talents and sets you free from emotional programming. It provides deep insights and removes tensions. It increases your awareness and eliminates prejudices while helping you recognize what's good for you and what's not. This stone helps you in every aspect of life. It brings abundance and career promotions, it connects you with your purpose, and brings you in touch with your true powers. It helps you reach higher states of consciousness more easily. It improves your self-confidence and authenticity. This gemstone helps supremely if you have any trouble with addictions, and it's used as a stress-relief stone too. It helps you break free from self-defeating attitudes if you have any, and it heightens your will and recharges your complete system.

Ametrine will help you if you're dealing with memory loss because it strengthens your nerves, stabilizes and corrects DNA structures, and supplies your body with oxygen. It improves your romantic relationships and helps you develop and maintain harmonious and healthy interactions. It synchronizes flow between the chakras and keeps your energy level equalized. It brings you more freedom and opportunities, and it helps you see yourself and others more clearly by removing judgmental thoughts. Ametrine helps you transform any disruption, imbalance, or impurity into healing energy, and it awakens your potential and connects you with high frequencies that you can use for your own good and for the good of others.

Morganite

Morganite is a stone of inner strength and unconditional love. It helps you calm anger and resentment. It has a gentle effect on you, dear Libra; it increases your gentleness and compassion. This crystal will help you heal your emotional traumas and losses because it brings you joy, pleasure, and deep peace within you and with the outer world. It activates your heart chakra and connects you with divine, angelic love. It provides slow and careful opening and healing of wounds, and it eases your pain. It's a nurturing stone that enhances feelings of love and light; it helps you maintain love, and it brings healthy commitment and care. It helps you get out of the trauma circle and enter into loving and soothing energies. You can overcome fears more easily. It heals broken hearts and painful memories from the past. It increases personal power, fairness, communication, and personal expression. It helps with mental problems and unfulfilled needs and desires. It releases you from stress and makes you more tolerant and understandable of others. Morganite improves your well-being and gives you a will to find a new purpose.

Blue Sapphire

Blue sapphire is also known as the "Wisdom Stone." It releases you from self-imposed limitations, and it liberates you from your inner cages and conditionings. It restores balance in your physical, mental, and emotional body. Blue sapphire releases you from unwanted thoughts and depression. It removes mental tensions and confusions. It can help you with lucid dreaming and psychic communication. It brings healing of emotional and mental suffering, and it gives you strength and focus by providing a better understanding of self. It makes you free to express your true feelings to others and share your opinion more openly, and it brings you more self-confidence and trust in your intuition. It resonates with your throat chakra and third eye chakra, bringing you serenity and peace of mind. This crystal brings great healing of any past traumas, even from past lives. It restores your health and brings abundance and prosperity into your life. It enhances your communication abilities, it helps you speak your truth, and it empowers you with inner vision. It helps you remember your dreams and seek for the truth.

Lapis Lazuli

Lapis lazuli means "Blue Stone." It's a protection stone, and it helps you open a gateway to your inner knowledge. It brings inner and outer harmony, which is your goal, dear Libra; it opens access to higher truths and encourages you to recognize karmic attachments and heal what needs to be healed. It brings you inspiration from other realms. It helps you calm the senses; it brings mind clarity. It also brings emotional calmness and stability. It increases harmony, honesty, and morality, which are your natural qualities.

This crystal stimulates the pineal gland, and it's connected with your third eye chakra. It brings great visionary powers and helps you connect with your inner truth and wisdom. It's a stone for spiritual growth, and it helps you reach a meditative state easily. It also improves your sleep and makes you enjoy your dreams. Lapis gives you courage to go after what you want. It relieves anger and brings you into sweet balance. It is helpful with headaches and body pains by bringing relief and relaxation and allowing you to rest and recharge. It improves your whole immune system.

Opal

Opal is a stone of hope and purity. It's your birthstone, and it brings you positive qualities of power and energy. It improves your vitality and endurance. It energizes your being and brings you positive thoughts. It helps you achieve synchronizations in all aspects of your life, and it stimulates growth and provides good sleep without nightmares. It keeps you safe from accidents and from negative relationships. It brings you good luck. It also improves your mystical power and visions by making you more confident and aware of your uniqueness. It brings you closer to your full potential, it provides freedom and independence. It can purify your kidneys and blood, it has great healing properties, physical and emotional. It brings you regeneration and clears your mind. It helps you trust your feelings and become truly self-responsible.

Clear Quartz

Clear quartz is a truth-enhancing stone. It's a stone of clarity, light, and reflection. It's known as a "Master Healer" because it balances and revitalizes your body, your mind, and your spirit. It amplifies your energy and intentions. It has a high vibration and it helps you connect with your higher self; it awakens your best potentials and allows you to live your life in its best possible version. It protects you from negativity of all kinds, it can relieve your pain if you place it on a painful part of your body, and it soothes your nerves. It strengthens your aura and clears your mind and body. It encourages you to achieve your goals. It helps you see the clear vision of your future, and it removes inner and outer distractions making you more open to receive the true image of yourself and your wishes. It stimulates your immune system and cleanses your organs. It enhances psychic abilities too and unlocks your memory. It helps you make the best decisions; it reminds you to reevaluate your choices and values and choose what serves your highest and truest qualities.

Blue Lace Agate

Blue lace agate calms your nerves and anxiety; it's a cooling crystal and provides a gentle sense of tranquility. It is an illuminating stone and empowers you with a strong sense of serenity and peace. It's a highly nurturing and supporting crystal, and it neutralizes anger and helps you sleep well if you suffer from insomnia. It's excellent for emotional healing. It harmonizes you and fills you with optimism and joy. It charges your self-confidence, gives you courage to express your thoughts and feelings verbally and helps you deal with difficulties; it brings a cheerful attitude towards life and relationships. It recovers you from injuries and suffering. It changes your perception for the better and encourages you to try things you never thought you would dare to try. This stone helps you carry on and deal with life challenges more easily.

It brings you patience and greater understanding of life, and it allows you to accept yourself for who you are and accept others too. It makes you more grateful and thankful, and it keeps your head cool and reminds you of the bright sides of life.

Black Tourmaline

Black tourmaline converts negativity into positive energy. It's a powerful protection stone because it keeps bad luck away from you and protects you from disturbing emotions and negative energies of others around you. It brings you better concentration by connecting you with your inner power. It increases confidence and inspiration. This crystal brings you relief from pain and boosts your immunity. It has high positive energy and brings you emotional stability and an optimistic view, calming anxiety and decreasing stress and tension. It heals you and protects you emotionally, physically, mentally, and spiritually. It's also good for protection from electromagnetic energies.

Black tourmaline keeps your body balanced, bringing the left and right sides of the brain into harmony. It also balances extreme emotions; it protects you from any kind of destructive energies. It purifies your surroundings from negativity and protects your auric field from attacks. It's good for arthritis, spinal pain and muscular issues. It releases you from any obsessive behavior. It quickly grounds you and keeps you protected from misfortune, sickness, and accidents. It is a wonderful stone for meditation and grounding, it helps you channel excess energy through your root chakra and release it.

Chiastolite

Chiastolite is known as a "Cross Stone" because it has a black cross formation when it is sliced. Its name comes from the Greek *chiastos*, which means cross marked or crosswise. It is also your birthstone. It brings you health and harmony, and it guards you from negative energies; it brings you emotional strength and accelerates your self-healing process. It has strong metaphysical properties; it's excellent for meditation, and it can open portals for you so you can acknowledge past lives' karma.

This crystal helps you deal with hard times and difficulties through your life, and it helps you face disturbing experiences and bring them out for healing. It helps you make the right decisions. It encourages you to get rid of any toxic feelings and thoughts and release old negative patterns. Chiastolite is a calming stone. It provides perseverance, strength, and power. It deflects and wards off any attacks, and it dispels curses and bad intentions. It keeps you safe from harm. It heals imbalances; because of this, it's great for nerves, rheumatism, muscle weaknesses, and blood pressure. This stone brings your whole body in balance. It encourages you to speak your truth. It heals your throat chakra while maintaining connection with your crown chakra and third eye chakra. It sharpens your senses and increases your intuitive powers.

New and Full Moon Rituals Using Ametrine

Ametrine is great for rituals and meditation during the moon phases. It will increase your concentration and keep you relaxed, guiding you into calmness; it will help you quiet your mind and connect you with planetary movement and energy.

Using your crystal during the moon cycles will enhance your potential and help you achieve your goals. It is your birthstone and it will harmonize you. Any meditation with it brings equilibrium between the body and higher self. Using ametrine continuously during new and full moon meditations and rituals will immensely transform your life in general. It can make you see life and relationships in a new light. You can release many stuck feelings from the past and even past lives, and you can carry out great self-healing and create new life for yourself.

Using ametrine consciously and intentionally will transform you for good, totally shifting your perception and understanding. It will bring you wisdom during your life, and it will make you use your own energies and come to awareness when it comes to your inner truth and your purpose here in this life.

You can cleanse and charge your crystal before these rituals. It can be cleaned with warm soapy water, but don't expose it to heat. You can recharge it under the light of the full moon.

New Moon

The new moon's energy is best used when you consciously work on your intention and meditate with your crystal. You should use this time to sink into your true self and set your intention from the heart. It's time for planting seeds and doing the inner work. It's time for beginnings and fresh starts; it's a perfect manifesting journey.

Wear your crystal or hold it in your hand. You can also place it on your heart or choose any body part that you think will work better. Choose your best position for relaxation and turn off any disturbing devices. Get away from noise and be quiet. Close your eyes, take a deep breath, feel your body filled with air, exhale, and feel how your body relaxes and releases. Continue doing this until you feel you're calm and centered. Now focus on your left and right sides of the body. Shift your focus from the left to the right and from the right to the left, feeling the symmetry and energy of your body. Juggle with your focus—right side, left side, doing this until you fully feel shifting from side to side, until you feel both sides, using your mind to focus on it. Now embrace both sides, feel the complete body, encircle it, hug your body with auric energy, feel complete and whole, keep this safe aura around you, feel as a whole with it. Set your intention; allow your aura to carry you in the direction of your wish. Feel the levitation. Trust in the process and let yourself go with it.

Your crystal stores all this energy work and your intention, keeping them safe and providing communication with the Universe so that your intention is ready to manifest. It keeps you centered and focused. It helps you keep the protective auric field and feel the whole body, left and right sides. When you let your intention out into the Universe, come back into your body to focus on your breathing again. Inhale and feel your throat, lungs, and stomach. Exhale and feel the release from the stomach, lungs, and throat. Continue doing this until you feel stabilized and harmonized. Feel the oxygen through you. Feel the flow of energy, tap into your center, and feel that you're everywhere. Slowly open your eyes. Don't make fast moves when you finish— just come back to yourself. You can write down your wishes in your journal. You can also write down how you felt during this journey.

New Moon Libra Affirmations

I am a beautiful and worthy soul
I allow myself to manifest what is best for me
I create the best version of myself
I have… (whatever it is that you want to have)
I trust the Universe and celebrate my existence
I manifest my heart's wishes
I have the power to transform painful experiences into wisdom
I honor my life and people around me
I respect myself and others
I am worthy of beautiful feelings and healthy loving relationships
I am aligned with the highest good

Full Moon

The full moon period is potent for releasing energy, things, people, habits, and anything that you feel uncomfortable with, anything that you find out of function, and anything old. You can free your blockages now. Use your crystal as a sacred tool during this phase.

Go into some quiet place so you can tap into your own inner quiet space more easily. Hold your crystal close to you, find the position which comforts you, and be still. Close your eyes. Focus on your breathing. Inhale, exhale, and become the breathing. Imagine you're the breath which comes in and flows out; feel yourself as an air wave that goes through the matter. You can go in any direction and you can move through everything; you can feel every cell of every creation. Wherever you feel any tension or disturbance, carry it and dispel it through the air. Collect from your body all the things that need to go and flow out of yourself as a breath scattering unwanted emotions, energies, and thoughts.

Being an air wave, you can go to any place, to the river, to the sea, to the highest mountain, to the rarest flowers. Collect healing drops of dew in the early morning. Absorb the essence and energy, going into your body and filling it with this enriched breath. On your way out, collect again toxic content and take it out as your body exhales. Catch this rhythm of being a breath which goes in and out through your inhale and exhale process. Use your imagination and intuition. Feel the power of being a breath and feel being free, ethereal energy that is limitless. You are free and unconditioned. Feel this freedom, getting rid of everything that slows you down. You are unburdened, so feel the lightness of being pure air; feel how it moves easily in any direction. Do this as long as you feel comfortable. When you finish, slowly open your eyes and keep the feeling of being a breath. You can keep this reminiscence alive within you and use it whenever you feel blocked or unable to move or make a choice. Your crystal helps you maintain this feeling, and it keeps your memory and allows you to step into this state whenever you feel you need it.

Full Moon Libra Affirmations

I embrace the truth
I appreciate my life path
I choose to love myself
I invite what is in resonance with my being
I know that everything is unfolding as it should be
I am supported by the divine
I let go of heavy thoughts and emotions
I let go of toxic relationships and people who are not
on the same wavelength with me
What I do, feel, think, and speak matters;
I am an important part of the whole
I feel peace and love from the heart of my being
and share it with others
I transform hatred into love, and I am an artist of life

SCORPIO

Scorpio Sacred Stones and Rituals

Scorpio is a water sign ruled by Pluto, god of the underworld, and Mars, god of war, symbolized by the scorpion, eagle, and phoenix. Scorpio rules the reproductive system and genital organs, and these body parts could create troubles throughout life. If you are born under this sign, you are deeply moved by your emotions. Your reactions come from the emotional center, and you carry the cosmic wound of death through your system; you hold this memory and knowledge of the transformational process: birth, growth, death, and rebirth. Your feelings are intense and magnified. Sometimes the intensity is so high that you can't express it. You have an affinity for the dark and underworld, for danger and the unknown; you want to investigate and research, you want to reveal what's hidden. You are attracted to secrets and everything mysterious, and you have a strong urge to go deep into the heart of the darkness and reveal it, uncover it, and find out what's in there. You want to find out what's so scary and mystical about it.

Your affirmations are "I TRANSFORM" and "I REMEMBER." You can experience deep emotional pain because you are so strongly attached to emotions. You have a long memory, and it can also cause you pain because you tend to repeat painful stories in your mind and relive them over and over again. You have a tendency to collect negative experiences, and you easily get addicted and hooked. You're probably not even aware of it. You're magnetically pulled toward the dark, and it's hard to explain to yourself why.

Your task is not easy, but you have enormous power and you hold potential to heal and transform. People might be a bit scared of you, but it happens for various reasons. Sometimes it's because they feel their personality mask is dysfunctional in front of you. You see through them and they can't face their own demons, or they feel naked in front of you. Sometimes they feel the intensity of your deep emotions which you carry inside, hidden, without expression, and they don't know what to expect; sometimes you vibrate so high with background feelings and emanate suppressed emotions which others cannot handle so well. This can make you an even more secretive and private person; it can make you unable to express yourself in front of others due to fear that others won't respond in an appropriate way to your statements, opinions, and feelings. You have to work toward letting go of these tensions. You have to learn the lessons from these built-up emotions and when the time is right, release them instead of collecting more and more of these negative memories.

You can be very possessive and jealous when you're too attached. You have to become aware of your power of transformation and use it in a constructive way. You can use these powers in a constructive or destructive way; you hold both ends, but you have to enhance your free will and decide how you want to use your healing and transmuting abilities. You know that "what you resist, persists." This is especially true for your sign, dear Scorpio, and you should learn to surf through the electromagnetic current of your wild rivers and become sorcerer and wizard of intuition. You can become a master of your own energies, learning the flow of chakras and helping others deal with difficulties and painful experiences. You have a gift to be a therapist. You can make great changes through changing yourself. You can be helpful to others when you learn how to accept and move on without holding grudges. You have to let go of revengeful thoughts because you have a tendency to think about an issue which happened years ago. You think about it for a long time and dedicate a lot of energy to it, which ultimately weakens you.

You hold great wisdom inside of your being, but you have to deal with lust, passions, instinctual habits, and attachments. You have to overcome and understand these levels of energy so that you can transform from Scorpio into an eagle and ultimately be reborn as a phoenix who rises from the ashes and the world of the dead. You hold the secret of initiation. You walk through the dark night of the soul and when you come out, the new dawn awaits you. Your heart is purified, as is your soul, and you can teach and help others go through this process on their own. You emerge from the battle. You are an alchemist; you are the healer. You hold the keys of transformation, and you connect sexuality and spirituality. You can transform lustful lower instinctual urges into high vibrational love and unity. There's nothing bad or wrong with instincts and desires. It's an experience through which you evolve and learn, and it brings change and wisdom through which you become your own healer. You learn regeneration and rebirth through confrontation with the unconscious.

You learn through surrender. You need deep intimacy and feelings of security. You want to be sure you can share your emotions with another without any fear of being judged or feeling exposed. You want deep connection and honest, meaningful conversations. You can achieve all that you want when you decide to let go of the perfect image you hold. You want a soul connection; you are magnetized by unusual things, and you're not afraid of taboo themes because you want to experience everything that's out of the ordinary. You make friends with fear. You learn that feeling is healing, so you release and transform. You have all that you need inside of you. You need to go through inner work and pull out what needs to be seen.

Crystals are super powerful tools for you; working with gemstones can help you immensely. Your natural potentials can bring outstanding results while using crystals. They have the power to transform and heal, as well. These entities are very important for protection and healing. Using crystals can make you more open to flows of new energy because they unlock your blocked cells and chakras. Crystals support your transformation and detachments, supporting the release of anything toxic or disturbing. They help you see things in a new way, and they bring you a new perception of reality and your true nature. Crystals vibrate with you and bring more love light into your life and surroundings. Their frequencies protect you and lift up your spirit. They help you get rid of obsessions, attachments, emotional pain, tensions, possessions, jealousy, suspicion, manipulation, and abuse of power. Stones will help you deal with losses, grief, complicated emotions, and confusions. With your pure intention and inner work, you can heal and transform any part of your mind, body, and soul.

The crystals that hold the best vibrations for you, which correspond to your energy and potentials, which help you harmonize and strengthen yourself in the best way, are malachite, aquamarine, smoky quartz, sodalite, golden yellow topaz, apache tear, black obsidian, rhodochrosite, charoite, and natural citrine.

The one crystal which is ultimately most helpful for you, Scorpio, is malachite.

Malachite

Malachite resonates perfectly with your intense energy and with Pluto. It promotes growth, change, and transformation. It has a strong healing energy and it's a powerful protection stone. It is connected with all chakras but mostly resonates with your heart chakra and solar plexus. It is known as the "Stone of Transformation," which is your greatest potential—to transform. Its message is to leave the past in the dust and move on. It helps you to go through this process of letting go and accepting the past in order to bring new beginnings into your life. It gives you courage to take responsibility for your life and become your own authority, to be in charge of yourself. When you feel emotionally wounded and damaged, this crystal brings you recovery and provides self-trust. Its deep vibrant green color has a hypnotizing effect. It helps you focus on new growth and break the bondages which prevent self-development. It empowers your spiritual powers and brings renewal; it balances the work of the chakras and helps you make these inner fountains of energy work in accordance to your level of perception and understanding. It brings you self-discipline and emotional control.

Malachite brings calmness to your thoughts, it helps you get rid of obsessions and emotional tensions. It awakens true love for nature and aligns you with nature's laws. It reflects your deep connection with nature and reconnects you with your true instincts and primal needs. It enhances your creativity and removes all kinds of blockages. It allows you to enjoy the beauty of life and the whole creation. It neutralizes emotional problems and brings you inner peace, it calms and brings relaxation. It is a very intense stone; if you find its energy too strong for you, you can combine it with rose quartz or mahogany obsidian. It has an antidepressant effect, balancing your ups and downs; it regulates your energy and helps you witness your emotions from a distance so that you do not get too attached to them. It gives you feelings of optimism, and it refocuses your view from negative to positive. It helps with blood pressure, arthritis, menopause, menstrual issues, asthma, epilepsy, fractures, joints, the pancreas, the nervous system and travel sickness. It has various healing powers. It boosts your immune system and absorbs negativity. It protects from radiation and electromagnetic pollution. It helps you with mental disturbances and encourages you to heal old traumas. It enhances loyalty, empathy, unconditional love, self-understanding, constructive transformation and peace. It stabilizes you when you feel emotional insecurity, it brings you inner strength and self-confidence.

Malachite also brings abundance into your life and it's excellent for manifestations and intentions. It is a deep energy cleaner which makes you open for new opportunities and helps you achieve what you need. It helps you reorient your heart's desire if you're heading into the wrong direction, it gives you sight through your heart, giving you new eyes to see what really makes you happy. It encourages you to open your heart for new experiences, especially if you've been hurt through past relationships. It reconnects you with your true purpose, it brings spiritual and material transformation, it helps you surrender and trust the process. It enhances self-esteem and extremely helps if you're shy or if you feel weak in some way. If you've been falsely accused of something, it gives you great courage to step up for yourself and speak your truth. It will help you identify your wounds and acknowledge your traumas in order to heal and transform your personality and life.

Aquamarine

Aquamarine is a blue-green crystal which resonates with water and the ocean. Its name comes from the Latin *aqua marina*, which means "seawater." It's the stone of courage and it stimulates self-expression. It's a calming and soothing stone, it reduces fear and anxiety, it helps you get rid of phobias. It brings clarity of mind, it gives clear perception, it tranquilizes overactive thoughts, it helps you get rid of mental confusions. It clears the channel between the throat and heart chakra, which helps you speak from your heart. It helps you deal with conflicts and disagreements; it will cool you down if fiery passion takes you over, it reduces stress and enhances self-awareness. It enhances your intellect. It promotes wisdom and knowledge. It can be used as a protection stone for travel on the water and as a protection against drowning. It empowers your communication skills. It helps you overcome judgmental attitude and increases your sensitivity.

Smoky Quartz

Smoky quartz is a powerful grounding stone, and it is an excellent stone for wandering minds. It brings focus and concentration. It neutralizes negative vibrations and enhances your drive and motivation. It helps you bring your dreams into reality; it is a strong stone for manifestation. It brings you emotional stability and calmness, it dispels fear and depression. It's connected with your root chakra and solar plexus chakra. It keeps the negative energy away from you and it greatly reduces any suicidal thoughts or tendencies if you have them. It keeps you safe from nightmares and damaging thoughts, and it helps you break bad and toxic habits.

Sodalite

Sodalite is a calming and grounding stone. It resonates with your throat chakra and third eye chakra. It unlocks your intuition and enhances intellectual abilities and memory. It brings you deep insights and connects you with your true desires. Sodalite charges you with more clarity and emotional balance. It brings you a deeper understanding of yourself and your truth. It encourages your mental capabilities and enhances logic; it brings you objective perception and calms your mind. It helps you pull out negativity from within and release toxic emotions and thoughts. It encourages you to express your feelings verbally, it balances your metabolism and boosts your immunity. It helps you achieve peace and calm excessive emotions. It brings serenity and makes you feel present in the physical world and body. It helps you accept difficult experiences and situations and brings self-acceptance.

Golden Yellow Topaz

Golden yellow topaz is one of your birthstones, and it resonates beautifully with your energies. It brings you abundance and prosperity. It's a golden stone which increases joy, fun, optimism, creativity, and emotional healing. It helps you achieve your goals and manifest your intentions. It is also a friendship stone and it attracts essential and helpful people in your life. It promotes loyalty and strengthens your faith. It assists your health and lifts your will. It is a powerful aura cleanser and brings you great confidence. It recharges your energy, brings you peace, and clears your path towards enlightenment. It brings you back to the right path, it helps you make the right decision which is for your greatest good.

Apache Tear

Apache tear is a gentler type of black obsidian stone. It brings deep grounding and comfort. It helps you recognize negativity and deal with it. It encourages you to face the danger and overcome depression. It's an empathetic stone and helps you go through periods of grief or struggle; it brings you graceful and gentle energy. This volcanic glass crystal helps you heal after difficult periods, tragedies, and losses. It empowers you with strength and courage to go through the self-healing process in the most nurturing way. It brings great healing during times of sorrow. It helps you accept your emotions and experiences and remove blockages. It will strengthen you when you're fragile, it offers gentle release of traumas, it infuses you with warrior-like energy, giving you motivation for life. It releases you from stress, it reconnects you with your inner guides and sources, it helps you deal with your inner darkness and leads you to self-acceptance. It provides great support during rough times and brings light to your life. It unlocks locked up energy and helps you unleash hidden forces; it brings old wounds out into the open and allows you to heal any kind of abuse you went through throughout life.

Black Obsidian

Black obsidian is an excellent stone for gaining self-control and psychic protection. It is connected with the root chakra. It brings unpleasant and negative emotions to the surface in order to transform and let go of them. It encourages you to face the truth and get rid of anything that holds you back. It stimulates your gifts and talents, and it brings you in touch with your true potential. It protects your aura, clearing negativity and creating a protective shield around you. It stimulates transformation, spiritual growth, intuition, patience, wisdom, and self-awareness. It provides security and releases you from any imbalances. It helps you release old attachments, such as old love and old burdening relationships. It helps you face yourself with honesty and self-love, it supports you while going through changes. It grounds your soul and helps you break toxic attachments and addictions.

Rhodochrosite

Rhodochrosite is your natural birthstone, dear Scorpio. It supports new beginnings, joy, happiness, and self-love. It encourages you to love yourself truly, to get in touch with self-care feelings. It's a great stone for meditation and emotional healing. It is a heart-centered stone and it has a loving vibration. It energizes your soul and opens your heart. It brings out forgotten memories and helps you heal any traumatic experiences; it brings deep healing of the inner child. It reconnects you with your childhood, it recovers and rejuvenates your well-being and state of joy. It strengthens your being and brings you feelings of self-worth. It awakens your forgotten talents and encourages you to develop your skills and gifts. It promotes selfless love, self-compassion, and self-forgiveness. It helps you let go of revengeful and self-critical thoughts, it brings balance to your energy fields, and it recovers your inner strength and connects you with your higher self.

Charoite

Charoite is known as a soul stone and a stone of transformation. It transmutes painful and negative feelings into healing. It stimulates spiritual growth and helps you accept the present, it opens your inner senses and helps you to find true joy in life. It will reduce your stress and worries, it helps you remove pessimism from your heart and mind, it improves your sleep and removes nightmares. It's a grounding, protective, and healing stone that provides physical and spiritual protection and healing. It encourages you to release deep fears, compulsions, and obsessions. It is a highly beneficial crystal and reminds you to create beautiful moments and memories which are worth keeping. It connects your heart chakra and crown chakra, and it encourages you to accept and receive love. It helps you remain calm and focused. It stimulates unconditional love. It lifts your vibrations and helps you achieve and maintain peace, patience, and tolerance.

Natural Citrine

Citrine is your traditional birthstone. It radiates positive energy and it enhances your confidence and creativity. It encourages you with honesty and decisiveness, it helps you get rid of emotional, mental, and physical blockages. It brings you abundance and prosperity, it helps you attract wealth and success. It brings you emotional balance and helps you deal with phobias and fears. It will protect you if you're surrounded with negative people, it keeps you safe and stable. It increases your intuition and clears your mind. Natural citrine is great for self-healing and self-improvement, it removes vicious thoughts and brightens your mind. It also helps you overcome physical illnesses, it helps you get up after a fall, it cheers you up and brings you great motivation, it teaches you to honor yourself and it keeps your mood high.

New and Full Moon Rituals Using Malachite

Malachite is very useful during the moon cycles because it has a deep healing effect when you consciously use its energies during the moon rituals. It also amplifies manifesting powers and enhances your intuition and insights. You can suddenly receive an image, emotion, or thought, or all three together while meditating with your crystal during the moon phases, which can help you solve your issues and heal past wounds. It can boost your confidence and stimulate your transformative and healing powers.

New and full moons are extremely potent periods that allow you to step into your inner realms and travel inside, opening new ways on your road and bringing you alignment between the body, the soul, and the spirit. You can use this time to transmute and transform energies in your favor and attract good things in your life. Using malachite during meditation under new and full moon phases will create new impulses within you and inspire you to search for a deeper meaning in every aspect of your outer and inner worlds. It can improve your life on all levels and give you fresh air and a taste of existence and your place in it. This can expand your mind and your insights, bringing you into alignment with the universal dancing rhythm.

Take care of your malachite and clean it often. Don't use soap, water, chemicals, or salt and don't expose it to sun rays for too long. You can clean it with moist cloth and charge it among quartz crystals. You can also run it through sage or incense smoke.

New Moon

During this phase of the moon you should use your manifesting powers to set your intention and initiate new beginnings. Combining a crystal with your energy on the new moon can bring you new birth and renewals.

This is a highly potent time to get you closer to your purpose and become more aware of your talents and skills.

You can place your crystal on your body or wear it, you can also hold it in your hands and just be aware of its presence. Find yourself a comfortable place and take a position which suits you the most. Make sure your body is in a position which makes you feel relaxed. If you feel any tension, try to find another position which is comforting for you. Close your eyes. You can play some calming healing music in the background, meditation healing tones are helpful to get you into a peaceful state. Focus on your breathing, let your mind be aware only of the inhale and exhale process, feel this flow, in and out, feel the expansion and contraction of the existence while you're breathing. Focus on your intention and be aware of the power of the crystal and the energy of the new moon. Imagine you're a point in an empty space floating and moving. As you move you stretch from a point into a line. Imagine you create your intention from this point, you shape your reality starting from this single point, you can draw anything, you manifest what you think. Follow the drawing line and shapes, follow the horizontal and vertical spiral, and feel the whole process of creating and drawing your intention.

You become this process of creation, you are intention, you are a point, you are a line, you are the triangle, the square, the star, you are the painter and the paint, you are the creator and the creation at the same time. Paint your intention. You are the viewer and the view itself, there's nothing that disturbs this process, you have limitless power, you are multidimensional, you create instantly, what you see is already created, no boundaries, no attachments, nothing and no one stops your movement. You are the wizard of your intention, you have all the elements encoded within you, you have the power to create your world, create your sky and clouds, create your day and night, imagine the unimaginable. Your intention is already manifested, you are already there. Remember the initial point from where this journey began, that same point is everywhere, that same point went through the whole creation and it exists in every part of the world you have created. That same point is you and you are everywhere. Wherever you look there's you, and from every point you can create and recreate, transform and reshape. The power of manifesting is in you. The crystal helps you become aware of your own power to create and to trust in the process, trust in your existence, trust in life, feel life, feel alive, feel the growth and changes. You can always start from this point. It is present all the time wherever you are and no matter what.

New Moon Scorpio Affirmations

I own the power to transform my life
I choose the way of how I want to live
My life is in my hands, and I am the master of my destiny
I co-create with the source of creation
I accept the outcomes that must occur to me
My potentials are endless
I trust that everything and everyone is exactly where they need to be
I am safe and secure; I trust the divine plan
I am renewed every day
I am strong, stable, focused, and self-reliable
I am ready to change, and I embrace the new me
I accept others for who they are, and I am grateful for being alive

Full Moon

The full moon is a time when you can experience extended and deepened insights, your emotions can go through some wild flows and it is the best time to use a crystal for grounding, self-care, self-healing, releasements, detachments, wound awareness, and discharge of painful memories. You can use it to release toxic patterns, to break the habits which are harmful. You can unblock stuck emotions and let go of obsessions and dark thoughts.

Have your crystal with you, hold it, wear it, or just have it near you as you do the ritual.

Take a position which makes you feel good and comfortable, close your eyes, spend some time just being and feeling, forget that you have a body and mind, just feel the being. Whatever thought or idea comes to you, ignore it, don't give it any attention, focus on being. Do this as much as you need until you feel the feeling of being. Whatever feeling comes, let it be, feel the feeling, let the mind bubble and let the feeling come into being. Don't let the mind occupy your feelings and take you over, let the feelings speak without you getting attached to them, let them express themselves. To feel is to heal, let the feeling become the healing. Let the old feelings come out and show themselves, let go of what needs to go, thank them for being loyal to you for so long, let them know you're aware of them, show your compassion and love and let them go. If the feeling is uncomfortable, listen to it, let it come even closer to you, it won't hurt you, you've already been through that, it just repeats the memory, it's not alive, it's long gone, all you have to do is let it go out through you.

Make peace with it. Don't resist your feeling, let it pass, open your heart and let it free, don't keep it locked in the cage, don't hold onto it, you won't lose anything, your essence is always with you, within you, in the now, it was, it is, and it always will be. Remember your true essence. Let the collection of pain disintegrate. Embrace your wisdom. Cry if you feel like crying, sing if you feel like singing, speak with yourself if your feelings want to speak, whatever it is that you feel, let it be, let it become your guide. You are an eternal being, your pain reminds you of how strong you are, you don't need to keep it in order to stay strong, you're already transformed, it's time to remove the damaging buildings and rise as a phoenix. Your crystal helps you go through this process. The full moon energy takes away what you no longer need; it's your death and rebirth process, and you're newly born and reborn. Fear is a feeling. Let it do its magic, but don't attach to it, don't give into it, just let it be.

Remember what you've been through, be proud of your path, become your own best friend, love yourself, be thankful for the good and for the bad, it's all just an experience which creates your journey and pours you with wisdom.

Full Moon Scorpio Affirmations

I forgive my past
I am ready to transform old wounds and
acknowledge the power that's within me
I have more than enough inner strength
and power to confront any crisis
I heal myself every day again and again
I let my traumas transform me, and I let them teach me and heal me
I see my attachments for what they are and I let go
Everything is always as it should be, there are no mistakes,
only lessons through which I learn to love myself more and more
I am brave and independent, and I know that the
Divine Source supports me all the time
Everything is possible in every single moment
I am the transformer
I transcend my limitations
I rise above after every fall, and I am resurrected through every
moment, growing into the greatest version of myself

SAGITTARIUS

Sagittarius Sacred Stones and Rituals

Sagittarius is the last fire sign in the Zodiac and is ruled by expansive Jupiter. It represents higher knowledge, higher dimensions of existence, vertical path, aiming high with an arrow, truth, philosophy, teaching, learning, and adventures. It holds principles of "I SEE(K)" and "I UNDERSTAND" and rules the hips, thighs, and upper legs. Being a Sagittarius makes you open-minded and adventurous, seeing things differently than most people. You own authentic perception, you're eager for knowledge, you're highly sociable and friendly, and you're able to make friends anywhere and from all cultural backgrounds, from homeless people to local shamans, vagabonds, police officers, presidents, businesspeople, people who live in tribes, all kinds of different people—and that's how your mind works too, it goes in all directions, it wants to know every experience, it's hungry for truth and meaning. You are naturally gifted with optimism, generosity, enthusiasm. You are a freedom lover, you want independence, you're thinking on your own, you have an explorative nature, you bring your visions and ideas to the world, you inspire many. You are connected with the mythological creature centaur and wounded healer Chiron. You bring wisdom and healing to mankind, you are the High Priest/Priestess, the teacher, you really hold the keys of all these potentials within you. Your mission is to unlock and awaken your gifts, give them purpose, expand and share your ideas and knowledge.

Because of your free-loving nature and free-spirited mind, you often can't stand being held down by anything. You tend to avoid your duties and you could become irresponsible and overindulgent. You can become talkative and philosophize too much on topics you don't truly know and understand, you can be overconfident and bring yourself into a lot of trouble because of it. You should avoid preaching and talking too much about subjects you haven't mastered yet. You can often hurt others when you speak without thinking about consequences, when you just say things no matter what. Even though you might be telling the truth, the truth is not always in every case scenario the highest good. The ultimate good is when you do no harm to others and yourself. You can still be sincere and truthful; you should emanate truth and kindness.

You should avoid extravagance and blind trust. You have a tendency to blindly follow someone's beliefs or someone who plays the role of a guru or a teacher. Your ideals could cost you a lot if you don't have enough maturity and you passionately and impulsively follow your desires without healthy reasoning. Your life is an adventure either way, good or bad, it's still an adventure, you have rich experiences from far and wide. Even if you don't travel anywhere, your mind spreads and collects various multilayered information, people, and circumstances. Your task is to bring these experiences to your awareness, to share your free-spirited energy with the world, to make a change and initiate motion in things that are stuck. You can suffer from lack of concentration, you can be restless and judgmental, your quick nature and curious mind can often wildly take you off the road and into the madness of uncertainty and agony. You own the greatest potential and talents for being the one who leads others in a true way, who knows the truth, who shares knowledge, who brings warmth and generosity. You want to explore the world and to be on a quest for truth. You should work every day on your self-betterment and turn your life into a true journey and dance between self-improvement, inspiring others, and experiencing wisdom through every moment. You have a straightforward approach to life, you want to find the meaning behind everything, you want true essence, you want to extract the juice of life from all experiences.

You want to visit foreign lands, to communicate with everyone, to get to know other cultures, to upgrade your knowledge day by day, you want to grow and gain spiritual knowledge. You are the gypsy, the student, the wanderer, your openness attracts all kinds of different friends and connections, you learn a lot through your interactions. You should avoid playing smart and talking a lot, or talking just for the sake of talking—you are much more than that, dear Sagittarius. You have a sacred mission here, so be present and aim high so that you can evolve into an independent yet loyal being, someone who owns personal freedom by being responsible, someone magnanimous who develops humanitarian qualities. In order to master these qualities, you have to overcome and face either through yourself or through others being judgmental, restless, dogmatic, fanatic in something, being unable to commit, careless, and addictive. All these things are also potentials that bring you good qualities and take you to a higher place.

Crystals will help you extremely to bring tranquility in your life when you need it, to motivate and brighten yourself when you feel depressed, to open up for new adventures when you feel there's nothing left to explore. It will improve your internal and external feelings as well. With your help and conscious decisions and intentions, crystals really work and respond. Sacred stones can increase your abilities to bring your instinctual nature in balance with your higher intelligence, to truly bring to fruition your potentials, to discover your hidden gifts, to develop your talents in a more productive way. Using crystals will improve your overall life, they protect you from various bad influences, energetic, physical, mental, and spiritual. They bring good luck, they refocus your mind in the right direction, they connect your lower animal nature with your higher self, bringing peace and order within your being. Your sign is half horse and half man, you are an archer and centaur, and crystals will empower your lower and upper nature awakening your true powers. Under your conscious work, they respond to you and bring you closer to your core essence. They will bring out what's not yours and give you a chance to release unnecessary grudges.

Crystals which are your helpers and supporters, stones which are your guides and which make you more free and responsible at the same time, crystals which resonate with you and bring you cosmic answers and awareness, crystals which are your intuition awakeners are turquoise, blue topaz, lepidolite, lapis lazuli, sodalite, pink tourmaline, iolite, vesuvianite, shungite, and sugilite.

The one crystal which works best with your energy and nature, the one which inspires your potential and enhances your willingness, is turquoise.

Turquoise

Turquoise is an encouraging and calming stone. It is your birthstone and it enhances your natural potential. Its color is characteristically green-blue, it reflects deep peace and compassion. It promotes adaptability, authority, future, and the truth. It brings you back into a state of trust and security, it helps you deal with troubles and go through the storm more easily, feeling protected and safe. It calms your body and soul during hard times and stressful moments, it brings you inner peace when you're disturbed, anxious, and nervous. It soothes you, it helps you relax, and it reminds you that rest is important. It gives you the ability to learn how to relax and regenerate yourself. Turquoise is the stone of wonders, it has energy of all elements within itself, it empowers your strength and flexibility, it enhances fearlessness and open mindedness.

It is also known as the "Stone of Warriors." It promotes courage, bravery, determination, and endurance. It provides personal protection and helps you focus on beautiful things in life. According to ancient legends, turquoise brings good luck when it reflects the light of the new moon. This crystal will inspire the creative sides of your personality, it will bring hidden talents to the surface. It will recharge your immunity and bring you more stability when you have to deal with anger, hatred, rage, or impulsiveness. It brings you balance and helps you find meaning beyond the material superficial realm so that you can develop a deeper understanding of the things and emotions within you. It encourages you to embrace your weaknesses and turn them into your lessons that eventually bring you wisdom. It brings you self-reliance and self-responsibility, it helps you become aware of the things that are blocking you and preventing you from becoming who you aim to become.

Sometimes you feel that you're aiming for nothing, but using crystals will bring you enthusiasm and hope to be more experimental, to give something a chance, to explore more and to bring your life into rhythmical dance synchronized with the cosmic laws and will. It will empower your presence and help you cleanse yourself from old wounds and past traumas, it protects your soul and your heart, it brings tranquility and empathy. This stone will protect you from panic attacks, depression, negativity, dark people and places, bad thoughts and bad behavior. It brings you insights about your past and future, it supports your visions and good intentions, it dispels fear and toxic emotions. It helps you bring poisonous and blocked emotions and thoughts from the past so that you can wash them away from your body and cell memory.

When you deal with impatience and want to act rashly and without thinking, this crystal will calm your instincts and get you closer to your intuition and higher feelings so that you can act from the place of wisdom. It also promotes wisdom and brings you mental clarity, it protects you on your travels and soothes excessive energy. It is a meditative stone too which can really help you when you're running around like crazy within your mind or physically; it will bring you the feeling of being here and now and helps you take a break to choose what's best for you in any given moment. It encourages you to speak the truth, to speak sincerely and gently, not hurting yourself or others. It makes you more aware of the words you speak and enhances your communicative abilities. It resonates with your throat, heart, and third eye chakras. It helps you realign your energy centers, it promotes abundance, and enhances your charm and charisma. It stimulates tissue regeneration, it has anti-inflammatory effects on your body, it purifies lungs and clears the throat. It boosts your whole immunity system. It promotes friendships and romantic love too. It stimulates self-realization and tunes you into your truer self, improving your life in many ways.

Blue Topaz

Blue topaz is your traditional birthstone—actually, any topaz is. It soothes and heals, bringing wisdom and truth. It increases your ability to communicate better, it brings clear communication. It helps you if you're distracted too much, it brings you forgiveness if you're struggling with inability to forgive, it enhances self-control. It helps you express yourself and increases your concentration. It helps if you're hesitant, it helps you make a decision and be clearer; it makes your words and thoughts clearer to yourself and others. It helps you if you have to make a public speech, it helps you if you're a writer, it promotes writing creativity, it removes creative blocks. It promotes learning and understanding and aids your spiritual growth. It also helps with digestion problems, anorexia and bulimia issues, and it improves your metabolism. It is very good for healing hurt feelings and calming the nerves.

Lepidolite

Lepidolite is a stone of transition. It brings emotional balance and awareness. It brings you change in a gentle way, without shocks. It clears electromagnetic pollution, absorbs the emanations, and clears the blockages. It removes negativity, it helps you maintain equilibrium, it releases you from stress and worries, it helps you accept yourself and others, it makes you accept life situations more easily. It stimulates the purification process, it detoxifies your body, it boosts your immunity, and helps with nerve pain. It rejuvenates and recovers your joints and its vibrations heal you if you're feeling exhausted. It also helps with epilepsy and Alzheimer's. It brings you stability and extremely helps you to handle tough situations and deal with angry people. It rebalances your brain functions, it protects you from nightmares, and helps you with depression and mental issues. This crystal encourages your independence and protects you from outer influences.

Lapis Lazuli

Lapis lazuli is a crystal which has a power to connect you with your higher self, to open portals for higher dimensions of your consciousness, which is something you already seek and which comes naturally to you as a Sagittarius. This crystal is sometimes called the wisdom keeper; it unlocks your chakras and connects you with your authentic self, it makes you aware of your knowledge and motivates you to aim and reach higher. It enhances your communication with spiritual guides and in ancient times it was seen as a stone of the gods.

It offers protection during an inner journey so that your inner travels go without evil spirits interfering and attacking you. It is also believed that this stone has a spirit of deities within itself. It makes you aware of your inner truth and inner power, it calms your senses, and its soothing effect opens your mind. It cleans your organs and benefits the respiratory and nervous systems. It removes destructive emotions from your system, it cleanses you physically, mentally, and emotionally.

Sodalite

Sodalite is your birthstone and it promotes wisdom, mind clarity, emotional balance, and intuition. It has calming energy, it is a stone of insights, it enhances your mental capacity and abilities, it unlocks and unblocks your closed and locked intuition, emotions, and perception. It will bring things to your awareness, it will make you see clearly your weaknesses and strengths. It encourages you to dive deep beneath the surface and find true meaning and core desires of your being. It removes chaos and confusion from your mind, it has the power to take you to the higher realms and see things from a distance. Its high vibrations recharge your self-trust and self-acceptance. It takes you to the places within you where you can achieve your tranquility; it empowers you with inner strength and bravery to face your own darkness. If you're on a path of truth and spiritual discovery, sodalite will be your guide and protector. It also regulates your blood pressure and balances your metabolism. It has a cooling effect and it's great for meditation.

Pink Tourmaline

Pink tourmaline is also known as rubellite. It has a lot of lithium inside of itself and it incredibly helps with depression and anxiety. It is a stone of love, self-love, and emotional healing. It increases your compassion and brings you great strength, it helps you heal emotional wounds. It radiates universal love and kindness. It helps you to move away from anything too extreme and gives you better perception and higher vibration. It is a natural healer for pain and suffering of the heart, for all matters of the heart actually. It heals your early childhood emotional wounds. It encourages you to leave any abusive relationship, it recovers you greatly if you suffer daily from anxiety and disturbing thoughts and emotions. It attracts joy, love, and optimism in your life. It attracts love in material and spiritual levels, it connects you with the earth and makes you aware of that connection between Earth and mankind, it makes you aware of the health of our planet. It helps you release any destructive feelings. It helps you repair yourself and brings you calm and peace. It provides balance in brain chemistry.

Iolite

Iolite is the perfect stone for activating and working on your third eye chakra because it is a vision stone. It is spiritually oriented and provides great intuition, visions and psychic power. It increases your inner strength and stimulates your imagination. It connects you with higher planes of existence and helps you do the shadow work. It encourages you to work on yourself and face your demons. It makes you ready to come down to the bottom and integrate lost parts of yourself in order to access higher knowledge and wisdom. It helps you if you have trouble sleeping and improves your dreams. It brings you inspiration, clears your mind, awakens your inner knowing. It empowers your deep inner work and helps you express your authenticity, and it removes fear from how others see you. It encourages you to be more responsible, it releases disturbance from relationships. It supports your growth as a human being and as a spiritual being, it aligns your free will with the highest good. It makes you be present in the now, in this very moment, enjoying it fully and acknowledging the true power from within.

Vesuvianite

Vesuvianite is a stone of strong vibration. It is a stone of support and it stimulates powerful effects on the one who wears it and uses it. It brings you closer to the true desires of your heart and connects you to the higher realms and higher self. It is also your birthstone and it works toward your personal growth. It promotes inner security, it is very strong for spiritual connection and battles with the ego, it helps you acknowledge your egoic wishes and desires and transcend them into higher knowledge and mental clarity. It removes anger and negativity; it infuses you with courage and makes you break the chains of any bonds that are imprisoning you or making you feel restrained. It helps you get rid of repetitive negative emotions and thoughts. This crystal brings you positive energy and feelings of loyalty, and it connects you more with your physical body and makes you aware of its intelligence.

Shungite

Shungite is believed to be an ancient stone. It is said it's older than two billion years, and it has many healing powers and various beneficial effects on a user. It contains fullerenes known as powerful antioxidants, and it's very good for physical health. It absorbs and eliminates anything that is damaging to your life, it protects you from electromagnetic radiation, it detoxifies your whole body and clears your mind from negativity and bad thoughts. If you're dealing with difficult and uncontrollable emotions, shungite will help you and keep you clean from any hard and destructive emotions.

It cleanses you mentally and physically, it protects you extremely, preventing negativity from forming around you and within you. It purifies your aura and your environment from destructive and negative energies. It is linked to your root chakra and is known as the "neutralizer" because it balances your left and right sides of the body, it brings you into your center and helps you maintain being centered. It has very intense energy and it should be gradually attuned to. It is a grounding stone too and helps you purify and shift stuck energy, and it transforms pain into wisdom.

Sugilite

Sugilite represents spiritual love and removes negative attachments. This violet flame crystal is very powerful for healing and protection. It is a strongly nurturing stone, it calms your mind and senses, it makes you aware of the present moment. It deepens your connections between the mind and the body, it brings you awareness and positive thoughts and feelings. It brings violet ray energy to the earth and its energetic vibrations bring you wisdom. It supports your third eye chakra and crown chakra, stimulating your inner visions. It brings you emotional healing and helps you release any stress and disturbances.

It's associated with spiritual growth and it encourages you to live your life more authentically. It reconnects you with your true passion and makes you live your truth. It is also known as the "Stone of Dreams," as it enhances spiritual abilities and reminds you of your soul's purpose. It makes you aware of the reason why you incarnated here and now in this particular body and in this particular place and time. It gives you answers to deep questions, it helps you receive answers, and enhances your intuitive powers. It helps you when you have to deal with grief and sorrow, it instills positive thinking and protects you from shocks, traumas, and disappointments. It brings you light and love in the darkest hours.

New and Full Moon Rituals Using Turquoise

Rituals during the moon phases are very potent and beneficial, especially if you use your crystal during the ritual. It has a very powerful force to manifest your dreams and intentions, to transform your life in a better way, to change your life, to help you solve key issues in your life. It is such a supportive tool that opens your mind and changes chemistry in you; it transforms your personality for the better if you use it consciously and with pure intentions.

Turquoise is very strong and powerful for meditation and its powers are enhanced during the moon phases. You can restore your balance through your physical, mental, and emotional body. Meditations and rituals with crystals are your superpower for enabling connection with your truth. New and full moons are extremely important periods in the month when we have a chance to enter the gap between the realms and improve and recover what needs to be improved and recovered in our lives.

You should clean your turquoise once a month, but don't charge it directly with the sun because it is sensitive to sunlight. You can cleanse it by smudging it, directing the smoke to your crystal. You can smudge it with cedar, incense, or sage and place the crystal through the smoke. You can also charge and cleanse it under the moonlight during the new and full moon phases. You can also cleanse it with your intention. You can put it in the earth for twenty-four hours if you have a safe place to do so.

New Moon

The new moon is perfect for meditation with turquoise and setting your intention during your meditation ritual. New moon meditation with your crystal is supremely energized and becomes very much alive, working with your energy and wishes and sending a direct message to the universal field. It raises your opportunities and helps your intention to manifest in the best possible way.

You should find some nice place for you on the new moon. Go somewhere where you feel good, some space of enjoyment and comfort where you can be on your own and get yourself aligned with the moon, crystal, and your intention. Sit down in the moonlight or stand, you can also do it in your room or any place you find comforting and relaxing to just be with yourself, or you can take a solo night walk before your ritual.

Find your best position and take your crystal with you, hold it in your hands or wear it on your skin. Sink into your open mind, imagine your mind expanding, hold your focus on your inner visions. Imagine you're running very fast, so fast it almost feels like flying. Run even faster than your fastest imagination. Your lower body takes the shape of the horse, you have a strong base and you feel unshakable, your strength overcomes any strength you've ever felt, you have this feeling that you can accomplish anything, your strong vital body is protecting you and your hooves are even stronger, carrying your whole body and being so grounded it feels like the whole world is under your feet. You run easily, your gallop is gracious and wild at the same time. You are the fastest being in motion and you feel the wind and dust behind your back.

You explore unexplorable lands, you run and stop whenever you find something that catches your attention. Go anywhere you want, through the fields, on the mountain roads, near the river or the sea, through the woods—explore every corner of the earth in your visualization. Your crystal enhances your imaginative powers and focus, you are projected in your vision. Your upper body is human and you have the ability to understand, communicate, exchange, interact, do whatever you want, speak with others you meet on your adventures. Make conversations, make friends, show places you like, take someone with you for a ride. This is your world, create it by your intention.

You carry fiery magic arrows with you, so shoot and aim up high, set your intention with true passion which keeps the flame of the arrow alive. You are the master of your world, you create your future, you have the power to change your past, change your story. Rewrite your life story, aim your flaming arrows of truth, watch them disappear in the heights and let them do their magic. Continue exploring and shooting as long as you want and feel good doing it. Your crystal will empower your intuition and help you achieve your goals.

You can use your journal and write down your experiences after this. Write down where you've been, what you've seen, who you've met, how you felt during your explorations, how many times you've pointed an arrow and set your intention. How did it feel? Do you trust yourself and your intuition? Were you indecisive about something or did you feel strong confidence? Answer these questions to yourself. Have a nice and calming conversation of truth with yourself after this meditation, enjoy your own company, and become your own truth and guru.

New Moon Sagittarius Affirmations

I am thankful for where I am right now
I am free and liberated
I am in touch with my deepest and highest desires
I know I carry inner knowledge within myself that
waits for me to be ready to unpack it
I am connected with my truth
I am aware of my inner power, strength, gifts, and intuition
I remember who I am
I am friendly, optimistic, unlimited, and authentic
I spread love, joy, and positive thoughts
I embrace the darkness and integrate all sides of existence
I fully trust life and I know that I am an important part of it

Full Moon

The full moon is a beautiful time for rituals with crystals. It will increase your will and faith in yourself and make you less stressed. Full moons often intensify your emotions, passions, and thoughts; they can take you off of your normal path and make you more emotional, angrier, more impatient, and sensitive. It is, therefore, very advisable to tune into your energy during this time and do some grounding, calm yourself, spend more time in your quiet mode, be still at least for some time so that you can clear your mind and heart and receive the true potential of the full moon's energy.

Sit down or lie down, take a position which suits you the most, make sure you're undisturbed and away from the outside noise. Focus on your breathing, feel the rhythm of the inhale and exhale, feel the whole cycle, feel the wholeness. Feel how the inhale and exhale is one breath as day and night is one day. Feel the unity. Calm your mind and body during this process, keep your focus here until you feel tuned in and centered, release body tensions and anxieties while you're doing focused breathing. Imagine pure light above your head pulsating and vibrating, feel the neutral energy of the light, feel its purity and always renewed life-giving energy. See this light entering your body through the top of your head, feel this contact of the light and your head, feel how it penetrates your body gently and calmly. Feel the light coming down and spreading vertically through your spine going through your chakras, enlightening and unlocking them. As you breathe in, feel this light spreading through your spinal column, creating perfect balance between the left and right sides of your body and brain hemispheres. It rejuvenates your whole system and gives new life and wisdom to your body, your heart, and your mind.

As you breathe out, take out all the garbage that's left after this washing away of light through your chakras and your spine, release all negativity and emotional wounds. Breathe out all toxic material from your past, anything that still makes you feel angry, unforgiving, rageful, anything that makes you feel sad, sorry, regretful, take it out and breathe in renewed, eternally youthful energy of light, watery and fiery light that cleanses you and recharges you completely. Breathe out again and imagine how everything blocked, stagnant, and persistent leaves your system and makes you feel lighter and easier. Repeat this process as much as you like, as long as you feel there's more of it, as long as you like it and find it soothing, as long as it makes you feel relief and liberty. You could receive important messages and insights during this process. Write down your experience when you finish and share your thoughts with yourself, be more intimate with yourself; these rituals open entrances to your higher self.

Full Moon Sagittarius Affirmations

I appreciate wisdom and allow it to come to me
I put my trust in my inner guidance
I am a true example to others, and I teach others
and lead them toward the highest truth

I inspire and motivate others to become their own teachers
I release and let go of painful emotions that still hold my attention
I accept my past and understand that
wisdom comes through all experiences
I honor my mind, emotions, and body
I am responsible and loyal
I am a true friend
My thoughts are constructive and beneficial
I allow everything that brings me no good to fall away
I expand and extend my experiences, my journeys,
my mind, and my soul
I bring good fortune around me and I feel abundance everywhere

CAPRICORN

Capricorn Sacred Stones and Rituals

Capricorn is the last of the earth signs in the Zodiac. It's ruled by Saturn, the lord of karma, the lord of the rings. Saturn's rings represent limitations and duties that we have to follow and honor in order to become self-mastered. Its symbol is a mountain goat with a fishtail; it's represented by a goat-fish or sea-goat. It is a paradoxical sign to a logical mind. The fishtail symbolizes primordial origins from the ocean and deep water, and the goat represents ambition, civilization, coming out from the abyss, and climbing the highest mountain to achieve goals and success. The highest expression is to master the self, to learn the lessons of being in the body, to gain wisdom from the deep waters and give it a form through endurance, self-discipline, and responsibility. It unites extremes, the bottom and the top.

Capricorn rules bones, knees, joints, skeleton, teeth, and the skin, and you being a Capricorn should take extra care of these body parts. Ruling these body parts also says a lot about being too rigid or strict in nature; you need to learn to be more flexible and fluid through life. This is one of your lessons, to be more adaptive and adjustable. Because this is one of your life lessons, life will throw at you many challenges through which you have a chance to experience situations that demand your wisdom of knowing what to do and how to do it.

Your lessons are tough and you probably have had to deal with many hardships since early childhood. This is because you have codes written in your blood and ethereal body of being mature before being grown up. You are premature and you can seem very serious to others, even gloomy. You mostly have a tough and heavy nature and attitude, you have an installed program within your mind to think that only the hard way works out, that nothing is for free, that in order to gain anything you have to work very hard. You are strongly persistent and you honor hard work, you know you have to earn something with your own hands. You are very determined and you can endure the toughest storms of life. You are reliable and you instill confidence in others. You are loyal and responsible towards your work, family, and friends. You have strong ambitions and you carry deep wisdom within your being, which manifests as dark and heavy energy while you're going through life being unconscious of your true power, unconscious of life and nature. This gives you feelings of heaviness and the feeling of carrying extreme burdens because it's hard to handle these old primordial memories and wisdom without being conscious of their energy and powers. That's why your task is to go through hard times to experience all turmoils and troubles so that you become aware of how strong you are, how much you can endure, and how after all the pain and troubles you're still here, you're still alive, and you still have a great sense of humor.

You are very humorous and your humor is very original and intelligent. This special perception of the world gives you enormous opportunity and power to renew yourself and others, to spiritualize matter, to become master of your destiny through seeing life and its cycles in a true sense. Being humorous is very close to being spiritual; you can't be spiritual without a sense of humor and this is something that gives you more power to endure everything and learn that life doesn't always have to be as hard as you thought. After you learn certain lessons you can release that need of always trying so hard to be good at something, to be of use and practice, to work hard in order to earn, to learn in a harder way, to have that worst case scenario in your mind, to always think that an outcome is not in your favor.

You also have a tendency to be strictly critical towards yourself and others, to criticize too much, even to make others feel miserable and unworthy. You tend to think and behave as if only your job and your life is important because it holds heaviness. You can be very rigid and strict, you can really damage your health by being in this state for too long. This doesn't mean that this is wrong, that you like making great mistakes or that you have to suppress your nature and force yourself to always be positive, no. You have to become more open-minded, more easy and lighthearted, but you can achieve this state only when you go through these feelings and experiences. You learn through them, you gain wisdom, you become who you're supposed to be, a wise elder, the hermit, the crone, your own authority, the true master.

You are patient, practical, and strategic. You learn the hard way, but what you (l)earn through your lessons stays with you through lifetimes, you crystallize it and carry it within you, it's yours and no one can take it away. Your sign corresponds with the beginning of the winter and it affects you deeply, you are melancholic, you have a serious attitude and older people influence you a lot. When you master your potential, you become the one who gives wise advice and serves as an example to others. You know solitude, you know hard times, you know cycles. You are connected with the symbol of winter solstice and it represents the rebirth of the sun, the end and the beginning of one cycle, transformation and alchemy, rising from the deep to the highest, growth and rise through your chakras, from the root to the crown, climbing Jacob's Ladder and returning to your source.

Using crystals will bring you many advantages and good things. You can improve your life through working with crystals, meditating and visualizing, intuitively communicating with them. You can prosper and bring the abundance you deserve in your life. You can help yourself incredibly and heal your pains and traumas. Using crystals with your conscious effort, with your nature and potentials, can make you more open to life, more accepting, more emotionally free. You have a problem with emotional expression and tend to seem cold to others. Stones can make you more unidentified with your personality and free to show your feelings to others, to express your inner world into the open. They will amplify your qualities and work to make them more evident and usable. Your bad habits and damaging tendencies can be brought to the surface so that you become aware of them and transform the way you live. Crystals are extremely powerful and they're alive, they merge with your energetic body and listen to you, they bring you more joy and happiness.

The crystals which work the best for you, the crystals which make you more of who you are and inspire the truth in you, the stones which get you closer to the source and to your goals are aragonite, garnet, galena, jet, azurite, magnetite, black tourmaline, and vivianite.

The one crystal which makes you available for self-mastery and self-improvement, the crystal which aligns you with others and with life circumstances, is aragonite.

Aragonite

Aragonite is your birthstone and it brings grounding, balancing, and soothing energies to you. It inspires you to seek enjoyment in life, to pursue true joy and good feelings. It provides encouragement and confidence, it teaches you patience and acceptance. It fosters the truth, and it enhances discipline and healthy boundaries. It is a stabilizing stone, it makes you more flexible and easygoing, it encourages a pragmatic approach to life which you naturally have, and it maintains it in a constructive way. It makes you more reliable and understanding, it clears your perception of reality. It is a nurturing stone because it enhances your tolerance and makes you more insightful. Aragonite takes you to the root of problems to see them and understand them, to accept them and heal them. It uplifts your emotions, it protects you from stress, and increases your concentration. This crystal stimulates connection with higher intuition and connects your thoughts with inner wisdom, making you available to express it and integrate it. Aragonite is an Earth Goddess stone, it deepens your connection with Earth and earth, with the planet and with the element. It increases your energy and increases your prayers, meditation, intentions, and affirmations. It empowers your senses and deepens your knowledge. It centers and grounds physical energies, it encourages your feelings of self-worth, it enhances your self-confidence, it brings back lost trust, confidence, and esteem.

It renews your strength and balances your energy fields, it brings you emotional healing, it provides gentle opening of the chakras. It supports your emotional growth and encourages you to find your center, to find that calm place that is always accessible and available for you. It brings you your sacred space and place within you, it shows you the way to your inner secret chambers of ancient wisdom. This stone frees you from anger and suppressed feelings, it meets you with the origins and roots of your traumas, fears, issues, and anxieties. It can get you back and face you with the true cause of your troubles, blockages, and sufferings from the past and from your childhood. It can give you deep insights of the source of your problems and heavy experiences. It brings love and peace frequencies to your heart and makes you more stable and able to relax. It accelerates your communication channels, it allows you to express yourself in a cooler atmosphere, through words, arts, voice, movement, or any other way of expression.

Aragonite is a great stone for self-healing. It brings balancing energy through your body, it's great for easing pain, it has a healing effect for muscle spasms and bones. It makes you feel comfortable in your body, it is helpful if you have a lack of vitamins A and D, it assists you with calcium absorption. It balances your brain functions and helps you with feeling too much responsibility. It raises your vibrations and connects you with higher energies and earth energy, making you feel grounded and stable. It helps you explore your past and childhood.

This crystal works as your teacher, it reminds you of your true source and of who you really are and why you're here. It offers you great support if you suffer from self-criticism or oversensitivity. It helps you to cooperate with others, to be a productive and meaningful part of the community. It helps you release your attachments and heal your emotional blockages. It brings up all things that you persist to hide and keep under the bed. It will speed up the process of facing your suppressed fears, emotions, memories, and traumas. It brings up to the surface those things you would rather avoid, and it brings you great healing through this inner work, making your inner space clean and clear so that spiritual development can enter truly and bring you closer to the meaning of this existence.

It is the perfect stone for resetting your body and your energy, it is a patient crystal, it calms your nerves. Aragonite encourages you to face your dark sides, to become aware of them, to meet them closely and to transform your life through this process. It helps you keep the right path through your life, it helps you not to take a wrong direction that could prolong your lessons and make you repeat some life situations again. It recovers your senses, it brings back will in your life, it makes you aware of the purpose of living and your role in life, it helps you understand your mission and duties. It expands your awareness and brings love light into your being, it reminds you that you are a bright shining star, it makes you understand the passage through the dark and void, it makes you see that facing the dark only brings you to the light and embracement of both within your being.

Garnet

Garnet is a deep, dark, red stone. It comes in more colors too but it's mostly found in a blood-red color. Its name comes from "pomegranate" which resembles the intense and thick color of the fruit. Since ancient times it was seen as a journey to the soul and as a stone which "glows in the dark" because of its protective properties. It has incredible manifestation abilities, it re-energizes you, it gives you vitality and increases the power of regeneration in the body. It brings warmth, blessings, wealth, and good luck. This stone enhances your self-confidence and eliminates emotional disharmony. It encourages healthy and balanced sexuality. It evokes the spirit of the fire and is also known as a "Hero Stone." It was also considered as a warrior stone protecting warriors from wounds during the battles. It regenerates DNA and purifies blood, it's good for the spine and bones, and boosts your immune system. It takes away your fears and worries leading you to the path of enlightenment. It energizes your life force and grounds your excessive passions and desires. Garnet keeps negative energies away from you. It sharpens perception of self and strengthens your survival instincts.

Galena

Galena has strong and powerful grounding abilities. It is connected to the root chakra. It brings great stability and brings your energies into alignment, gently opening new paths to wisdom and awareness. Its strong vibrations enhance your will and encourage you to face any challenges on the way. It clears and aligns your chakras, it brings calmness and clarity to your physical and mental states. It makes you feel as if you're weightless, it releases you from unnecessary and heavy emotions, thoughts, and memories. It absorbs negativity and transforms it into healing and uplifting energies. It enhances tolerance and peace, and it empowers you to acknowledge and embrace sides of yourself that kept you in fear for many years. It helps you to overcome self-limiting beliefs, it helps you break unhealthy patterns, it makes you see yourself and others from another point of view. It supports self-transformation. Galena is a stone of harmony, it helps you to maintain motivation and courage through life, it brings you wisdom of seeing fear as a natural emotion, and by knowing this you're given access to higher paths and awakening.

Jet

Jet is a form of petrified wood; its origin is organic. It draws out negative energies from your aura, it releases you from unreasonable fears. It relates to the root chakra and connects you to the earth's energy. It is a magnificent grounding and protective stone, it has highly purifying properties and it can be used to cleanse other crystals. It brings you great healing if you've been a victim of a traumatic experience. It alleviates grief and sorrow, it protects you from violence too. It helps you understand your lessons, it helps you see the purpose and deeper meaning of negative experiences you've been through or you're going through. It is a wonderful stone for dealing with deep depression and mood swings. It protects you from illness, it encourages you to release stored pain and blocked emotions. It's said that it has the power to control evil entities and keep you safe from their attacks. Jet eases the pain of a broken heart and soothes the pain of being separated or losing someone close. It stimulates your psychic abilities and motivates you to join the path of self-discovery.

Azurite

Azurite has a strong influence on your mind and brain functions; it has strong vibrations and it encourages you in your "pursuit of the heavenly self." It enhances the flow of energy through the nervous system, it supports you to meditate and it's brilliant for work on activating third eye chakra. It removes illusions from your mind and heart, it strengthens your memory and enhances your intelligence. It reconnects you with the Universal mind. Azurite stimulates lucid dreams, astral projections, insights, visions, and imagination. It helps you use your intuition in the most productive way and guides you on your spiritual path. It cleanses you and aligns you in order to help you through your inner journey. It brings you new perspectives and stimulates your memory, it brings back lost memory too. It purifies you from fears, sadness, phobias, chronic worries, and stress. It inspires you to achieve and actualize your greatest version, to give birth to your light being.

Magnetite

Magnetite is a wonderful manifestation stone because it helps you attract things that you desire the most, it has natural magnetic energy. It activates your entire chakra system. It is a grounding stone and it balances the hemispheres of your brain. It is a stone which balances polarities, it creates healing vibrations on all levels. It helps you recognize dualities around you and it makes your masculine and feminine principles interact in a healthy way, aligning you from within and releasing chakra wheels from blocks. It gives you a new perception of yourself, it helps you see yourself differently, in a new light and with different qualities. It eliminates confusion and obstacles; it removes burdens and keeps you safe from negative energies. It encourages motivation, confidence, endurance, and tenacity. It was known in the past as a Shaman's stone. It brings you back lost faith and inspires you with truth. It makes you trust your intuition and use it to your own advantage. It helps you remove unhealthy and unsupportive situations and people in life. It helps you release and cleanse yourself from long buried fears, attachments, unforgiveness, and pain.

Black Tourmaline

Black tourmaline is extremely protective. It is associated with your sign and aligns very well with your energies. It is considered to be a highly electromagnetic healer. It strengthens your will, it encourages you to accept changes and shocks in life, it empowers you to go through a personal transformation process. It enhances your emotional stability and makes you more flexible in expressing your true feelings. It brings your buried memories and pain out on the surface so that you can release them and free yourself from blocking energies that prevent you from self-improvement and soul evolution. It is the perfect stone for protection, it brings you great purification and detoxifies you from negative thoughts and emotions. It makes you aware of everything unhealthy within you, it brings you closer to yourself, and makes sure that you pass through every damaging and destructive pattern that's left in your mind and heart. It strengthens your immune system and brings you a positive attitude. It helps you release pain, emotional and physical. It purifies and transmutes negative energy around you and keeps you safe from attacks. It's a great stone to hold in your hand and just feel its positive vibrations, which can be too much for you if you have a lot of negativity to deal with, because this stone will bring it out in the open for you to meet it.

Vivianite

Vivianite is another birthstone of yours, dear Capricorn. It brings peace and serenity into your life. It emanates vibrations of love and brings you healing of deep emotional wounds. It helps you acknowledge and remove inferiority issues; it is a powerful healer and it reminds you how to heal yourself. It stimulates your body's healing process and it is great for healing anemia because it contains iron. It shouldn't be exposed to the sun for too long and it shouldn't be displayed too much, it's better to keep it away from exposure. It inspires clear communication and brings you mental clarity. It awakens feelings of compassion for yourself and others. It is great for teeth and bones. It reduces pain and helps you recover if your physical body has been injured or traumatized. It releases any negativity from you, it revitalizes you completely. This crystal improves your overall health, it takes away unwanted vibrations from you. It unlocks your heart and purifies your auric field. It will liberate you from feeling uncomfortable in your own skin, it will help you embrace yourself in a beautiful way. It is a stone of peace, love, compassion, and spiritual awakening. It will help you go through any difficulties; it helps you make a needed change in heavy situations. It makes you see life from the heart center and align with it. It awakens your heart vision and boosts your self-esteem.

New and Full Moon Rituals Using Aragonite

Moon phases are known to be magical times for inner work and connection with the worlds beyond the physical senses. New and full moon energies transmit and emanate special ingredients to each soul on this Earth and it is incredibly beneficial if you work with your crystal during these phases. Your willingness and intention in interaction with your sacred stone and moon's energies will bring you various new insights and solutions that are crucial for your soul and your life in this physical reality.

Aragonite is extremely powerful. Its frequencies will probably bring out on the surface your emotions, fears, anger, and any unresolved issues and traumas so that you can heal them. It will assist you during your meditations and under the full and new moon phases it will be of even greater support to you.

The best way to cleanse and charge aragonite is to use the energy of the earth. Water should be avoided, and you should keep it dry. You can put it on the ground while the sun is up but don't do it for too long. Make sure that the ground is dry. You can also cleanse it with sage smoke or your breath and energy. Be careful of using it directly after charging because it can dig up stored emotions from your being and spiritual challenges.

New Moon

During the new moon you should focus on your intention and your image of your future self. You should concentrate on your well-being, thinking about how to improve your life and bring more true quality to it. Being a Capricorn and using aragonite during the new moon is supremely beneficial; you are an achiever, you work to accomplish your goals, and this energy will boost and speed up manifestation for you. This time is extra potent for planting seeds and you should use it to meditate and work with your crystal.

Direct your thoughts toward what's the best for you. Find a calm and peaceful spot where you feel completely safe and secure, a place where you know you can just relax without expecting anyone or anything. Be alone with yourself in the quiet of space and time, feel the calmness of being here and now wherever you are, feel that place within you which lives in complete peace and abundance, stretch yourself to your own center. Close your eyes, take a deep breath and feel the oxygen through your nose, feel your thoughts being refreshed and renewed. Exhale slowly through your mouth, repeat this until you feel lulled into this rhythm. Feel your thoughts and emotions, they will come to you immediately: images, distractions, questions, maybe you'll even want to quit doing this meditation, but hold on, sit with it, listen to yourself. What do you hear? Let them be here with you, don't push them away, these are entities that live within you, and you're cleansing yourself whenever you spend a little time on your own in the quiet. You will hear your inner noise, let it be.

Don't force anything, just allow it to pass through you, to go through you, to express itself and say what it has to say. You will feel great relief soon, don't give it any attention, just let it exist without interfering. Focus on your forehead, focus on the place between your eyebrows, focus your mind on your third eye chakra, feel it as if you're touching it, feel how it pulsates. Whatever comes to you, this pulsation will dispel it if it's negative and absorb it if it's good for you. This is your ultimate tool and your crystal enhances its powers. Focus on your intention and vision, feel it moving through you as an energetic etheric rope, feel and see your intention climbing to your third eye chakra and let the pulsating embrace your wishes, let the vibrations send your intention and manifest it for you. Trust your inner guides, let the energies do the work. You sent your message through the most reliable medium, you sent your post and it will be delivered instantly. There's no before and after, only now, and you feel this as you feel your third eye chakra spreading its light energy as a fountain all around you and within you. Sit with this feeling for some time and enjoy pouring energy which embraces you wholly. When you feel good enough, when you feel you've felt all that needs to be felt, slowly open your eyes and sit like that with yourself in peace and calm.

New Moon Capricorn Affirmations

I attract goodness in my life
I allow abundance and allow myself to
feel good without feeling guilty
I understand that when I'm encouraged,
all others around me feel encouraged too
I am aware of my influence on others and
I accept being more responsible for myself and my thoughts
I allow wonderful life to happen to me
I am aware of life and its miracles
I appreciate that I'm alive
I appreciate all the people who went through my life,
those who left, those who are gone, those who stayed,
and those who are yet to come
I welcome all the changes and transformations that are on my way
I accept life's challenges and
I am ready to become the better version of myself

157

Full Moon

The full moon brings the greatest opportunity for you to release pent-up emotions, to liberate your inner self. You have an extremely potent chance during every full moon phase to cleanse yourself and face your darkest parts. Sometimes it will feel very intense and you'll go through a big emotional discharge, other times it might pass unnoticed, but there's always purging going on through this cycle. Your crystal can help even more with breaking your blockages and taking out what was hidden in the deepest roots, it takes you to the cause of the cause. You should cleanse yourself during this phase, take care that you eat easy food, avoid alcohol and drugs, avoid any medications that put you in a certain state. Be clean with yourself; as you cleanse your crystal you should also cleanse, charge, and prepare yourself for the ritual. You can go somewhere in nature since you're an earth sign to connect more with your element. Do some grounding before your meditation. Through healing your inner wounds, you also heal your physical body. Your thoughts and state of mind dictate your physical health.

You can take any position you want. Lie down or sit down, choose a comfortable place for yourself, make sure you feel good and relaxed. Prepare for the ride with your inner child and inner wounds. Close your eyes and sink into your darkness. Remember, no matter how dark it feels, there's always the same amount of light within you. This is your purging process. Let your inner child guide you through these dark chambers and show you where he/she is wounded. This is a perfect time to deal with unresolved feelings, sufferings, losses, and grief. Anything that disturbs your present has its cause in the past, and by awakening your inner child you release your growing process and start maturing in the best way. By acknowledging your inner child, you awaken your soul's journey and become your own authority. This sets you free. Facing yourself will bring you the ultimate feeling of easiness and freedom.

Go through the dark chambers, walk the halls of your life, the doors are unlocked during this process, you can enter any room you want and see what awaits you there. Maybe you have unresolved conversations you need to have with someone from your past, maybe it is with someone who is gone, but here everything is possible and you can manifest anyone or anything. Visualize and imagine whatever it is that you need, nothing is impossible in this world. You can fly anywhere, you can dive and run, you can be any animal, plant, element, or person. You can be all at once. Feel the courage and support you have from energies and your crystal, everything supports you on this path of releasing, any struggle and challenge is presented now so that you overcome it. This makes space for self-realization and the full moon makes sure that all that needs to be seen during this phase comes to you one way or another. Receive these messages that are brought to you now, don't resist them, just receive them gently and with peace. Let them guide you and protect you and let go of what needs to go. Don't push away, gently accept it, feel it, heal it, and release it. Repeat this as long as there's material for releasing and as long as you feel you should. After this process, stay with yourself for some time, contemplate and recapitulate what you went through.

Full Moon Capricorn Affirmations

I initiate and accept healing powers in my life
I release feelings of guilt, and I release all
damaging thoughts from my being
I let the light come into my existence and show me the way
I am truthful, prosperous, and fearless
I am an artist of my life, and I create the greatest art of it
I let go of critical thoughts and words,
and I speak with love to myself and others
The energies around me and within me are taking care of me,
they do what's in the best interest for my body and soul
I recognize my talents and allow them to be born and expressed
I cherish my wounds and pain, and I am aware of their importance
I allow true growth from within,
and I welcome the blossoming of my essence

159

AQUARIUS

Aquarius Sacred Stones and Rituals

Aquarius is the last air sign in the Zodiac and also the last human sign besides Gemini, Virgo, and the upper body of Sagittarius. The ruling planets are Uranus and Saturn, which makes it an even more complex sign since Saturn and Uranus have very different natures. They come together in Aquarius, the Water Bearer, which integrates both planets within and has a task of awakening and liberating. Aquarius rules ankles, shins, calves, blood circulation, currents through the body, and electromagnetic field. Being Aquarius makes you sensitive to these physical and ethereal parts of your being, you are connected with electricity and water, thunderstorms, lightning, and enlightening. You seek ultimate freedom and brotherhood feelings between humans. You carry deep desire of the Soul to be liberated and free from any conditions, free from all limitations that are inherited and imposed on mankind through our history, false education, past traumas that we carry in our DNA as a memories which we're unconscious of but which prevent us from normal functioning as a complete human being.

You can be seen as a weirdo by the majority because you don't fit into the regular social rules and patterns of society, laws, and systems. You are attracted to new ideas, new ways of doing things, new techniques of healing, everything that is original and out of the ordinary. You love unconventional people, you rebel against any rigid laws, you are passionate for your freedom, but you can be resistant to change. You're often forced to change through some unexpected and shocking situation. You love independence more than life itself, but at the same time you have a strong desire to socialize with others. You love being friendly and being in harmonious relationships, but you want to keep a detached, objective attitude too. You're afraid of losing your own authenticity through relationships. You can become paralyzed when it comes to expression of your feelings, you can suffer from frozen emotions and have issues of becoming too intimate with others. You can be afraid of giving yourself away to someone because you have this very strong need for being your own self and out of this fear you tend to avoid relating closely to others. You can become careless and cold, a distant and apathetic person. You can become a stranger even to yourself sometimes, and others can perceive you as dark and odd, someone who doesn't give a damn about anything.

You could also become attached to your friends and switch them with your family, run away from your family and start living with your friends. This is completely fine, and you are given this nature and characteristics for a reason; it is through these blockages that you learn important lessons and go through transformative processes. It is through this struggle that you become more open and flexible with showing your true self, with sharing your emotions and becoming more of who you are. You have objective qualities for a purpose, without it you would never be able to experience freedom, you wouldn't be a potential awakener of the human soul, you wouldn't have the ability to bring innovations, you wouldn't be allowed to detach from your personality and meet your essence. You would be stuck in personal identification and taking things too much to heart, then you wouldn't be in a position to express your eccentric and unique qualities, you would never be the one who influences others in the most extraordinary ways, unexpectedly. You love through the differences and that's why you can connect with the most different people and unite them. You bring together those who are completely opposite in nature, culture, tradition, race, color, habits, and anything else that defines somebody.

You love to merge what is incompatible. You don't like being stereotyped, you never follow the crowd, you are unpredictable and you're very sensitive to injustice. You follow your own rules, you have your own priorities. You want to experience as many different things and people as you can in life. Your rich experience brings you wisdom and you serve others through being the original you, unselfishly sharing and connecting. You learn through life that you were actually collecting limitations during your fights against them instead of liberating yourself from them, then you understand that these were the greatest lessons through which you truly reclaim your power and freedom. You learn through blockages and conditions, you fight them, you feed them with your attention, and you understand one day you've got all that you need to break free without any fight, you just become aware that you were blocking yourself and that you're ready to try a different way. Without this fight and rebellious nature, you would never come to know this. But when you acknowledge it, you see that you don't need it anymore, you can be whoever you want to be without any obstacles in your way.

You bring rise to consciousness; your intelligence and experience together build wisdom which you pour onto others. Your ideas are inspiring and future oriented, you encourage others to awaken their souls, to become true Humans, to stop obeying rules, to follow their own rhythms and to be in accordance with the Cosmos and nature. You want to find the truth in everything, and you start seeing the Source through everything around you and within you. Your task is to give knowledge a form and pass it to others, pass it for the generations which are coming after you.

Crystals are beautiful, alive crystallized energies. They're transformative and life changing for the ones who use them. You can help yourself outstandingly using crystals. They work with you and for you, they are synchronizing with your energy and nature. Crystals tune in with your life, with your past, with your habits, and they have the power to show you what's wrong with your life. They bring out what's hidden from your usual sight and awareness to help you see where there's work to be done. They open channels for transformations and bring you insights which guide you towards improved life, towards purposeful and useful experiences. They sync with you and support you in daily routines and with your relationships, with your inner journey, your family, your wealth and health.

The crystals which are infinitely helpful for you, which magically influence you and exceptionally transform your life are angelite, amber, red garnet, aquamarine, albite, merlinite, fuchsite, rainforest jasper, and larimar.

The one stone which is the best for your progress on all levels is angelite.

Angelite

Angelite belongs to your sign, dear Aquarius. It is the perfect healing stone and it brings you mastery of all kinds of communications. It is known as an "Angel Stone," it reconnects you with universal wisdom and knowledge, it relates to throat chakra and brings healing and unblocking of it. It is also known as a "Stone of Conscious Awareness," it recharges you completely, it enhances your self-expression, it purifies you and makes you open for angelic communication. Angelite expands your consciousness and dispels feelings of anger, rage, and sadness, it creates a protective field around you and defends you from fear of the unknown. Angelite is your spiritual guide, since you're a sign of truth seeking. Angelite makes sure to keep you safe on your path, to keep you protected from all kinds of attacks, to keep you away from possible psychic drain, to protect you from visible and invisible entities. It heightens your perception and brings you into conscious contact with angelic realms, it makes you available to communicate with your higher self, to enter the higher realms of existence and pour wisdom from the waters above into your physical body. It brings your physical body into alignment with the ethereal network and makes it possible for you to communicate telepathically. It is said that if two people are apart, if they each carry a piece of angelite, they can connect through telepathic connection.

Since it is connected with the throat chakra, it gives you a voice of truth, it brings you clear and clean communication, it makes your expressions more powerful and meaningful through words, thoughts, songs, melodies, singing, using mantras, AUM singing, mind communication, communication in your dreams, inner dialogues, inner speech, inner voice vibrations. Being an Aquarius makes you naturally open to new technologies, electromagnetic field healing, music healing and frequency healings, and angelite extends and supports you in these areas, it brings you fresh visions and ideas, it enhances your original creativity and motivates you to bring them into manifestation. It brings you closer to your personal inner truth, it protects you and helps you with astral travels if you're experiencing them. It offers you pure and divine thoughts and emotions, it brings you releases of earthly bonds in a healthy way. It transmutes your pain, it awakens compassion, it brings you calmness and peace, it releases you from unnecessary stress and worries. It beautifully brings you acceptance of things you cannot change, it protects you from cruelty and prevents it from happening. It can bring you deep tranquility if you work with it and ask for peace and guidance, it encourages you in every way and makes you be more self-protective and self-responsible. It balances you and your communication. Through healthy and balanced communication, your whole life changes and aligns with the truth. Your emanation transforms and instantly the whole reality around you changes too. Angelite also reshapes your reality through changing your perception and awareness.

It is a dreamworld stone too, it's great for lucid dreaming and it protects you from attacks during your sleep and out of body experiences. It connects higher and lower vibrations, and it strengthens your third eye chakra and makes the flow run freely through your chakra system. It regenerates you physically, emotionally, psychologically, and spiritually. It relieves you from physical, emotional, and mental pain too. It helps to get rid of prejudices, brutal behavior, and cruel intentions. It supports you greatly when you deal with life challenges, it recovers your emotional body from suffering of all kinds. It is excellent for higher knowledge and awareness, it inspires you to learn astrology and ancient science, universal mathematics, universal language, and everything that brings you closer to enlightening. It enhances your psychic abilities and makes you more self-forgiving. It brings you knowledge of symbols, it connects you with divine messages, and gives you access to akashic records. It brings you deep insights and makes you read the symbols and interpret them in the true manner, which is extremely helpful for your life and understanding your place and purpose in it. Its properties are many and you can only benefit from using angelite. It helps you with physical healing, it's great for infections, it balances fluids in your body and recovers your throat. It balances thyroid glands, it regenerates your blood vessels, it corrects deficiency of hemoglobin. It brings renewal and repairment to anything which has degraded.

Amber

Amber is your birthstone and it goes along with your energies. It is electrically charged when rubbed and this energy has a super healing influence on your body. It is a grounding stone for higher energies. When you feel excessively energized or like you're going to fly off, this stone will soothe your energy and calm your nerves. It is an excellent cleansing stone, it cleanses your mental, emotional, and physical body, it absorbs and transforms negative energy into healing and positive frequency, and it protects you from too much high electric energy. It helps you connect with the present moment and keeps you balanced. It brings you inner wisdom and helps you develop trust and peacefulness. It absorbs pain and helps you eliminate it from the body. It brings you clarity of thought, patience, romantic love, purification, calmness, and endurance.

Red Garnet

Red garnet brings regeneration and revitalization, it enhances your sexuality in a constructive and healthy way. It balances your root chakra and heart chakra. It controls anger specifically toward the self. It protects you and strengthens you. It is a stone of commitment, it brings you feelings of love, warmth, devotion, sincerity, trust, and understanding. It is believed that it warns you of upcoming dangerous situations, it promotes courage and survival, and it is great for working with kundalini energy since it's connected with the base and earth chakras. It brings soothing and calming energy to your feelings and it removes emotional disharmony. Red garnet is an energizing and cleansing crystal, it creates and keeps strong and balanced energy within you. It supports you in the process of releasing, it brings damaging old emotions to the surface and prepares them for transmutation. It brings you a positive flow of energies through your body.

Aquamarine

Aquamarine is a stone of courage, illumination, and empowerment. It emits calming energy and its name means "the water of the sea" which makes a perfect match for your energy as an Aquarius—even your names are similar. It quiets your mind and clears away confusions, it sharpens your perception and intellect and makes you see the bigger picture. It was carried as a talisman against drowning and it was carried by those who traveled on sea. It promotes self-expression and reopens your inner ocean, and it unlocks unexplored places within you and enhances your intuition. It helps you learn and master your lessons, it illuminates hidden causes of things that happened or that are happening to you, making you more aware of the truth and more ready to accept certain situations from your life in order to let go and heal. It uncovers your emotional patterns that are blocking and preventing you from true self-expression. It supports you if you're dealing with feelings of grief, depression, and sadness. It helps you see other sides of the same thing, it encourages you to face yourself and open up your psychic abilities. It helps you if you're dealing with dependency of any kind. When you feel helpless and desperate, Aquamarine will support you immensely to see that point of view from a different perspective and move on with a clear mind.

Albite

Albite eliminates the fear of the unknown, giving you courage and confidence to confront hidden and forgotten fears. It connects you to the psychic self and amplifies your intuition. It supports personal freedom and it's connected with your crown chakra. It boosts your mentality, it stabilizes brain wave transmissions, it has great healing properties with bi-polar disorders. It purifies your energy and aura, it brings healing to your mind, it helps you think more clearly and logically. It gives easy flow to your relationships, enhancing cooperation and healthy interaction. It stimulates your mind, memory, intelligence; it brings your thought processes in order, it helps you see things in a true way. It is great for learning; it inspires you to gain more true knowledge from the Universe. It reminds you of your self-worth and brings you emotional stability. It has been used to treat eye disorders, circulatory problems, emotional issues, and stress. It is very helpful if you're feeling low mental energy as it gives you strong mental focus.

Merlinite

Merlinite is a shamanistic stone. It stimulates deep intuition, psychic knowledge, and spiritual development. It opens you up for receiving higher impressions, it improves your inner visions and insights. Merlinite attracts potent magic and can help you recall past lives. It increases your self-mastery abilities, it supports you to discover your shadow-self and face it, it encourages you to embrace the unknown sides of yourself in order to become whole. It works as a catalyst stone for spiritual journeys and it has a power to remove veils of illusions, introducing you to profound intuitive abilities and potentials that are locked and hidden behind these veils. It connects you to mysticism and offers communication with the spirits and souls. It makes you aware of subtle energies around you and within you, it reveals your deepest intentions behind all desires, it reveals your unconscious motivations. It is known as a magic bearer and its name merlinite is associated with the wizard Merlin and it attracts mystical experiences. It motivates and inspires your interest in astrology, tarot, numerology, runes, symbolism, and all things that relate to magic and mysticism. It transforms negative aspects of lower vibrations into positive and constructive energy. It is a stone of self-mastery, it encourages your dream world and dreaming, it is a stone of wizards and alchemy.

Fuchsite

Fuchsite is a stone of rejuvenation and renewal. It is known as the "Healer's Stone." It helps you restore feelings of joy and happiness in life, it brings you emotional and psychological balance. It brings healing of mental issues, eases the pain, and soothes you. It makes you accept and embrace life more easily and it facilitates the inner journey process and helps you if you're feeling overwhelmed. If you're dealing with too many tasks and schedules, fuchsite will ease these duties and help you get more organized. It will enliven the inner child within you and reconnect you with your true and original self. It makes you more aware of self-care and self-healing, it increases self-responsibility and it helps you discover the root cause of your problems.

It gives you a fresh new perspective of life if you're feeling down and have a lack of will. This crystal reminds you that you have to take good care of yourself first. If you find yourself doing too much for others, giving too much service and not protecting yourself, fuchsite will encourage you and make you aware that you need to step back and let others take their own responsibility. It promotes growth and expansion and stimulates problem-solving, miracles, blessings, and ultimate healing.

Rainforest Jasper

Rainforest jasper has a subtle energy and it provides joy and happiness. It connects you with the heart of nature and makes you aware of the connectedness between every living thing in nature. It reminds you that nothing is separate and that we're all interconnected with all that surrounds us. It makes you aware that we're all integrated into one big living organism, that we interact with all things around us. That animals, plants, earth, grass, sea, trees are all part of the greater whole and that we as humans wouldn't be able to survive without all these elements. It connects you with Mother Earth and her wisdom. It makes you aware of feeling joy through existence and pleasure of being alive and experiencing the world through all its beauties and wonders. It connects you with nature spirits and elementals. It strengthens your physical body and calms down your emotions, it infuses you with vibrations of peace and love. It restores faith and makes you more heart centered. It motivates you to take action and do things that you were avoiding.

Larimar

Larimar is a high vibrational stone with soft and gentle healing frequencies. Known as the "Atlantis Stone" and the "Dolphin Stone" because of its ocean-like qualities, it can connect you with ancient energies of high technology civilizations like mythical Atlantis. It awakens ancient wisdom and extremely high potential to heal and enlighten all the bodies within you: emotional, physical, mental, and spiritual. It emits high energy which enables you to fiercely look inward and face yourself. It brings tranquility to the heart and mind, and it brings you strength and confidence. It dispels phobias, panic attacks, stress, and fear. It teaches you how to love and respect yourself in a true and beautiful way. It increases self-nurturance and self-respect. Larimar strengthens your inner self and enhances emotional stability, it encourages you to speak from the heart. It is one of the "spiritual stones" that introduces you to new dimensions.

It is an earth-healing stone, it possesses feminine healing energy, it restores connection with nature and with the Goddess vibrations. It brings great harmonizing healing energy to your heart, mind, and the body. It brings you feelings of trust, it helps you heal yourself from past traumas and even wounds from past lives. It helps you tune into a meditative state and release any stress. It brings you peace, love, and tranquility through making you ready to step into self-healing and self-love.

New and Full Moon Rituals Using Angelite

Using angelite anytime is extremely benevolent, and during the new and full moon phases, these potentials and energies are amplified and heightened even more. You should use your crystal always, and during these moon cycles your intentions and healing processes will be supported magnificently. Moon phases and crystals are very connected, and you can easily synchronize with the wisdom of these energies while meditating with angelite.

You should use these phases to go into a meditative state using a crystal which will support you on this journey and make you receptive of love, kindness, compassion, forgiveness, friendliness, communion, and all things that one human being should experience and feel as a natural emotion instead of something that's out of reach. Feeling fear and loneliness is also a natural emotion and angelite will help you to accept all these emotions that you're feeling, it will support you and encourage you to integrate all sides of existence and accept yourself fully. During these meditations with a crystal under the new and full moon, you are gifted with the greatest opportunities to heal yourself from all the pain and traumas you hold, from all things unconscious and unseen that are suppressed deep in your subconsciousness. You are offered to start your life from anew, to transform what you don't find constructive and to attract things which are beneficial for your health, your life, your family, your whole existence.

Before the meditation you should cleanse and charge your crystal. Don't use any liquids with angelite since it is a very soft stone. Don't wash it with water. You can charge it under the moonlight by placing it on the ground or burying it in earth. You can cleanse it with smudge by running it through the smoke, you can use tuning forks if you have them. You can also use a soft cloth to clean it. It can be cleansed and charged through your visuals, intention, and breath. You can use Reiki or charge it under the sun and under the stars too.

New Moon

The new moon is your perfect timing for new beginnings and meditation using angelite. It is a fantastic time to do something good for yourself and your future. It is very important to initiate something positive during the new moon and to let go of the things that are blocking your energy and true feelings. This period is amazing for you to tune into cosmic energies within and receive wisdom from your inner storage, to unlock your secret powers, to refresh and restart.

Hold your crystal or wear it on your skin. Take any position you like, you can sit in a chair or on the floor or outside on the ground or on sand. You can lie down if you want. Feel free to experiment and find your ideal position for meditation. Close your eyes and take a deep breath, then slowly exhale; repeat this a couple of times until you feel your heartbeat is calm and your mind is ready to tune into an inner journey. Feel your body, listen to what it has to say. Are there any aches, itches, disturbances while you're trying to stay calm? You'll probably feel some of it but don't worry, it is completely natural to feel it, continue breathing and feeling yourself.

When you feel you're ready, imagine yourself being a beautiful translucent blue wave, feel your new body and texture, feel the quality of your movement, feel the motion and the soothing color of your being. You're moving gently, sliding through the sea, you are an eternal and everlasting wave. As you disappear with the surface of the sea you emerge and rise again in a new place, you're always present and unbreakable, you're flowing and receiving guidance from the Source and divine wisdom. You are one with life and existence, you're transforming all the time. In one moment, you're small and sparkling; you feel the vibrations of the water and your structure. In the next moment, you're huge, gigantic, you're crashing and merging with the water. You're foaming and splashing the shore. Feel every version of the wave under all conditions. Feel how you're splashing and intertwining together with other waves. Feel how you're moving forward with them in the same direction. Feel your strength and force under the stormy weather, feel the wind moving you and giving you direction. Feel your connection with all elements, feel your fearless nature under the thunderstorms, feel your night motion and moonlight reflections in you. Feel the speeding up of your movement, feel what makes you move, feel oneness with everything. Feel your transparency and mirror-like body. Embrace your wisdom and motion, embrace the feeling of being who you are.

Set your intention and let it surf on the waves, let the wind carry it, let the wisdom which is beyond the visible take it over and transfer it further to manifestation realms. Trust the process, trust the waves, trust the wind, trust the earth, trust the water, trust the all-knowing center which is

within you. Let your intention flow freely, don't hold onto it, just set it and let it go with the cosmic awareness. Feel the beauty of yourself, feel the brilliant dreamy energy, feel the pleasure of being alive here and now. Enjoy your journey.

Remember this experience and let yourself feel the joy, feel all the feelings, feel all of it. Remember that you always have access to this, you are all of this, you are the whole existence and you are co-creator of all the life you see and feel.

New Moon Aquarius Affirmations

I have all that I need to improve my life and myself
I am ready to receive what's destined for me
I am supported in all that I do, and I trust my guidance
I allow the Universe to fill me with wisdom and abundance
I accept the gifts of the divine, and I am aware that
I am an inseparable part of existence
I know who I am, and I know that I am becoming
the best version of myself
I feel love through all that surrounds me
I accept the world and people as they are, and I am aware of the
importance of each human in this reality
I feel inner strength supporting me all the time
I welcome the changes and transformations,
and I welcome whatever comes;
I trust in myself and in my path

Full Moon

The full moon is such a great time to work with yourself in order to draw out anything disturbing and challenging from your system. It is that super potent period when you have a chance to release and let go, to receive wisdom and profound information about your life, your destiny, your emotions, your past and future, your traumas, your childhood, and your past lives. It is also a time when you can cleanse yourself and discharge from negative emotions and memories. Full moon rituals with angelite for you is a wonderful opportunity to step out of toxic and dysfunctional patterns, to enter into essential presence. This is the best time to squeeze out essential oils from your being.

Close your eyes and get yourself into a nice and soothing position. Take any position you find comfortable, any position that makes you feel the least pressure and tension. Let your body breathe on its own, let it relax without your interference, don't let your mind disturb it, don't listen to your mind, let it chit-chat and listen to your body. Your body has its own intelligence and wisdom, let it do what it knows, let it show you its knowledge. Allow yourself to receive this knowledge.

If you feel resistance in your body, just keep breathing with your eyes closed and concentrate on physical feelings, they will tell you and show you all the emotional and psychological issues you hold, it is all connected. Your body carries all your traumas, all your memories, good and bad. It knows your emotions, it knows your reactions and habits, but you forgot how to listen to it, you mostly listen to your mind and mental intelligence. Stay on your own with your body, feel how it moves while it breathes, feel the skin and how it protects you, enter into body language. Let it speak and express itself, let it dig up what's ready for release and transformation. Travel through your body, energize each part of it, step by step. Start from your toes and go all the way up to your head, feel each toe, energize it with your attention, focus on the feelings that you get while you do this. Feel your feet, ankles, your calves, knees, your whole legs, your abdomen, each finger on each hand, feel the energy and the current through it, feel the emanation.

Continue energizing your body parts, feel the waist, the forearm, do this for each side of your body, left elbow, right elbow, then both together, do this for all parts on both sides. Feel your whole arms, right and left shoulder, stomach, chest, throat, neck, your back. Feel your chin, your mouth, your left and right nostrils, your whole nose, left and right cheek, left and right ear, left and right eye, your forehead, top of the head, back of the head, your whole head. Make sure you don't skip any part. When you go through your whole body part by part, feel the oneness of it, feel the whole body at once, let the feeling overwhelm you, let yourself become this whole, this unity, feel the body holy and wholly. Feel your aura, feel how it emanates and let it dispel all the noise, disturbance, negativity, fears, anxieties, and depressive thoughts and feelings. Feel how it protects you and refreshes you. Angelite will be of terrific help and support while you're going through this journey, you will be motivated and encouraged to do it.

You will feel extremely relaxed after this meditation, you will feel your body differently than usual, you will see it from a completely different point of view, you will enter into a deeper connection and communication with your body and your life will improve outstandingly.

Stay with yourself for some time in the same position when you finish this practice, just be and do nothing. Slowly open your eyes when you're done and welcome the new you.

Full Moon Aquarius Affirmations

I know and I remember that everything is possible
I allow myself to go through painful memories and let them go
I understand my life's challenges and why they happened, and I
wouldn't be where I am today without them
I am grateful for life that I am living and experiencing,
and I am thankful for being alive
I allow changes and I am ready to recreate my life
I am the one who has the power to create anything that I need
I am powerful and strong, and I have the ability to
accept my past and create my future
I owe nothing to anyone but to myself; I am fully responsible
and I choose maturity on all levels
I accept joy and happiness, and I allow true connections with others

I am not afraid to express myself openly,
and I show my true emotions to others
I am in love with life and I am aware of both sides of it;
I know that in truth everything is experience, be it good or bad
I am the wizard of my life

PISCES

Pisces Sacred Stones and Rituals

Pisces is the last water sign and the last sign in the Zodiac too. The twelfth sign is an incredibly important number in symbolism and mysticism. Pisces is for numerous reasons associated with the mystical world, with the otherworldly, all things timeless and absolute. It's a sign which is in this world and out of it at the same time and is ruled by Jupiter, lord of expansion and magnifying, and Neptune, lord of mysticism and transcendence, lord of the oceans and unseen depths, dissolution and rebirth. Pisces rules the feet, lymphatic system, immunity, and mucous membranes. As a Pisces, these parts are sensitive and you should take care of them, either they serve you supremely or they cause you troubles. You carry ancient keys within your being which can unlock your original self and others around you when you go through needed life lessons and transcend your limitations and attachments. You hold the affirmation "I BELIEVE." You are the believer of the Zodiac, but often you can have issues with belief too because of it; both extremes can work.

Your sign is represented by two fish swimming in opposite directions, but they're connected and linked, they go together through the cycles of lives, they're bonded, swimming between the spirit and the matter. One fish is directed towards the heights, to the vast Universe, to the skies above and the other is directed to the depths of the ocean and unexplored. Subconsciousness and consciousness, veiled and unveiled, seen and unseen, you carry the seed of your whole life, you embrace within your sign all previous signs and experiences of the Zodiac wheel. Your temperament is fluid and sensitive, you often feel like a sponge, absorbing other people's feelings and emotions. Emotion is energy in motion, and you are made of it, your codes are mostly made of these elements, you are water but not any kind of water, you integrate all waters within you, waters above and waters below. You easily pick up others' moods, and that's why others often see you as someone who is moody, but you actually absorb the emotions of those around you and you suddenly become someone else. That's why you often feel confused, you take over their state of being and you're not even aware of it, it happens without your intention. Fluidity and absorption of emotions is something you have to go through and learn how to accept without being too attached to your feelings. You learn through life how to detach from these feelings, they're your teacher and guide but they bring you pain and suffering. You often feel victimized and betrayed by others or by the world. These are all experiences which you have to go through, these are your exams that you need to pass and master.

You have the power to transcend all these emotions which are huge and unspeakable. There's a great spiritual wisdom and growth behind these struggles and sufferings. You learn through them and you master your element of water, and by mastering it you become master of all elements. Every one of us has these abilities within ourselves, it is through Pisces archetype that each of us goes through to include and encircle the whole. Each of us has all signs within ourselves and each is important. Through Pisces we surrender to the divine and come back to the source, we return to unity, to oneness, which is beyond our logical understanding. Being a

Pisces isn't an easy job and you could have a lot of issues and struggles when it comes to being a part of the whole, which is your primary nature. You already are a part of the whole and you know it, but because of your totally different approach to this material world, you could face a lot of obstacles on your way. You can easily decide to quit something, to escape from this reality and forget about it. You want to escape through dreams, drugs, alcohol, medications, hallucinations, visions, imaginations, paintings, poetry, music, dancing, any aspect that provides feelings of not being here, not being present in a sober mind.

You are attracted to all of these things and you could become an addiction victim through your life. These are all huge lessons and teachers for you. When you overcome your addictions and attachments, you become free, you become your own master of dreams and wishes. When you go through different kinds of addictions, be it through people, things, arts, or anything that's already mentioned above, you break from your boundaries, you transcend this illusion of material boundaries and unite two fish into one. Your multitalented personality and expressions then come to true realization, then it becomes your true reflection, then you do it out of love and not out of the need to break free and hide behind it. You do it because you enjoy doing it, you learn who you are, and you share your inner genius. You learn that you don't need to save others, to save the world, to save the planet. You don't need to take over somebody else's pain and suffering, you don't have to be a victim, you don't have to sacrifice anything but your own limitations and sufferings, which will fall away naturally once you learn what needs to be learned.

You hold the principles of infinity, spirituality, all things boundless and universal, you seek for the soul, you seek for ultimate union and you have the power and mission to achieve it. You have psychic abilities, your impressions are true art, your mission is to turn escapism into transcendence, trance and dance. You show others and yourself that the eternal one is expressed and reflected through many and that it remains eternally connected with its source where it comes back after the dissolution of the matter so that a new cycle can begin.

Using crystals as a healing, protective, meditative, spiritual, and physical tool is very important for you, dear Pisces. Crystals are enchantingly beautiful, their colors and energies are haunting, they provide mystical energy and healing to the one who uses it. You can benefit so much if you consciously wear it and meditate with it, you can come to a greater understanding about important life questions and situations that you're in. You can help yourself while using them because they activate through you, they activate and tune in with your energy and temperament. They work to align you and bring you to a true Self state. You can improve so many life aspects if you work on yourself and use the power of crystals for self-healing and attracting good things into your life. If you use them truthfully and with pure intention, crystals will respond accordingly and bring you many gifts and take away what needs to go. They serve you and work towards balancing your whole body, inspiring and encouraging you to express yourself honestly and to bring more self-love and love for others in your life. Your questions will become more meaningful and you will start receiving needed answers as crystals are alive and have soothing and healing frequencies.

The crystals which are the most valuable for your nature and soul, crystals which can bring you true visions and understanding, crystals which can open your inner sight and set you free from false limitations, crystals which bring you closer to your true mission and understanding of yourself and others are coral, amethyst, bloodstone, smithsonite, sugilite, diaspore, African turquoise, aegirine, and natrolite.

One crystal which works the best for you and provides the most, according to qualities which are in sync with your energy and potential, is coral.

Coral

Coral is very appropriate for you and it is associated with your sign. It comes from the ocean and it is known as a "Sea's Garden"—it comes from the garden of the ocean. This name is also connected with past belief that it was a plant. It holds the ocean's energy and transfers soothing and calming vibrations to you. It has unique healing, protective, and metaphysical properties. It is not a very popular stone, but this makes it even more mystical and charming which suits your energies very well. It calms and quiets your emotions when they're too agitated or when you feel overwhelmed. When you feel like you're losing it all, like you're losing control over your feelings and behavior, coral will support you and bring peace within. It comes in a variety of colors and it has various influences. It is known as a stone of peace and transformation, and it is also known as a stone of mystics. It brings you harmony and stability to your inner self. It helps you enjoy life. It makes you see life from a brighter point of view and accept what you couldn't accept before. It opens your mind and expands your awareness. It enhances transfer of knowledge and connects you with spiritual masters and true ancient mystics. It helps you become more involved in this reality and receptive to the gifts of the outside world.

It brings you understanding through connecting you to spiritual realms and makes you more positive towards this life that you're given here in this 3D reality with your physical body. It makes you more willing to enjoy and learn through this life of the matter instead of resisting it and avoiding it. It helps you deal with anxieties, paranoid thoughts and emotions, panic attacks, irrational fears, and inner conspiracies that could ruin your life and your friendships and relationships in general. It brings more life into your being; it reconnects you with life itself and connects you to the past knowledge through which you can gain wisdom and personal freedom. It charges you with bright energy, it increases intuition, imagination, and visualization. It awakens and opens your mind's eye, it brings you deep and profound insights, it invokes the power of the Source within you. It reminds you of who you are and fosters creativity, courage, healthy self-expression, unconditional and platonic love. It has high protective frequencies, it absorbs negative energies, and brings you the deepest emotional healing since its home is in the water, which is your ruling element. It promotes wisdom, immortality, and happiness, it stimulates the richness of the mind and removes brain fog and mental confusions that you often struggle with. It helps you in making sober and wise decisions, it makes your mind aligned with your heart and emotions.

Coral will clear the path from any confusions, smog, unclarity, ignorance, uncertainty, doubts, clouded thoughts, and presumptions. If you're skeptical about something, coral will bring you into a calm state. It is a perfect stone for meditation and stepping into the zone of oneness within. It makes you aware of your place in the external and internal world. It reminds you of your true gifts and talents, it awakens your inner genius.

It prevents loss of energy and protects you from any disturbing and negative attitudes from the outside. It protects you from heavy emotions which come from others around you, it keeps you shell-protected because it has qualities of a shell. It has great protective qualities and it takes care of you. It stimulates sensitivity and adaptability. It makes you feel safe and feel at home wherever you happen to be. It brings you a comforting feeling that everything is and will be fine, it protects you from uncooperative people and those who could overburden you with their troubles and traumas. It keeps evil influences away from you, it gently confronts you with your shadow side and kindly makes you prepared for facing your subconscious parts.

It strengthens your circulatory system and your bones, it is used for tissue regeneration and improving the nervous system. It helps with disorders of the spinal canal and thalamus; it is also used to help with arthritis issues and anemia. It cleanses your organs and can be very beneficial while battling mental illnesses and mental instability of any kind. It brings recovery and regeneration after a long illness and dispels depression.

It helps you to really listen to what's being said to you, it helps you to see the signs and listen to the people, nature, senses, inner voice, and the Universe. It encourages you to release damaging thoughts and emotions, it makes you aware of what is destructive and what is good for you, it helps you see the truth and motivates you to live a better life, a life that you truly deserve as a human being. It reminds you that you're here for a reason and it brings you closer to truly see with your inner vision and wisdom what that reason is. It balances your chakra system and brings stability and better orientation through matter, energy, time, and space. It brings you inner transformation and insights, it aligns you with the cosmic laws and rhythm, it brings you revival and purification. This stone will infuse you with healthy altruism and inspire you to take action where it is needed. It offers you the greatest chance of breaking the habits which are draining you and making you fail each time you get up and collect yourself after a long time of picking yourself up. It makes you stable and strengthens your will, it won't let you fall into pieces again over the same lessons, it will help you see the patterns and transform them. It offers you a permanent shift from toxic habits which can be mental, emotional, physical, or any kind of habits. It reminds you to breathe, it protects you from chaos and disturbance, it eases the fear and reminds you of the slow motion, it reminds you to tune into a calming rhythm of breathing which brings you into a meditative state instantly. Coral will confront you with your personal mirror and make you see all the inner ugliness that's left to be transformed and released. It makes you a master swimmer and diver through the ocean of life.

Amethyst

Amethyst is your traditional birthstone and it is considered to be a master healer. It is very popular and has many associations. It is said that it prevents drunkenness, which is why it suits you well too, since you can be prone to escapism through alcohol amongst other substances. It calms excessive and destructive passion; it brings peace when you're overwhelmed and feel that you can't take it anymore. It prevents a tsunami of rage from happening, since you can put up with a lot for a long time until something totally meaningless triggers you one day and you burst.

Amethyst protects you from inner and outer destructive forces, it improves sleep and removes nightmares. It strengthens your immunity and can be used as a pain reliever. It is great for the development of all sides of your being, it protects you from bad thoughts of others and it brings you purification of past suffering and pain. It makes you aware of unhealthy patterns and helps you let go of them. It is supremely good at cleansing energy and bringing soothing vibrations. It enhances meditation and opens you to the higher self. It connects you with realms which are beyond this one.

Bloodstone

Bloodstone is your ancient birthstone, and it helps you regain your personal power and talents. It stimulates intuition and creativity. It is considered to be a hero's stone and it awakens true courage within you, it makes you decisive and self-assured. It makes you brave in dangerous situations. It protects you from unhealthy desires and helps you rebuild yourself after times of despair and turmoil. It helps you see the positive sides of hardships and inspires you to break old habits and make room for healthier ones. In ancient times it was always connected to blood detoxification, it was used to improve circulation and to heal warrior's wounds. It recharges your active side and infuses you with the needed courage to confront challenging people or situations. It increases your overall vitality and physical energy; it brightens your perception and revitalizes love. It brings mind clarity and understanding to confusing situations. It is tied to the root chakra and it provides primary feelings of security and groundedness.

Smithsonite

Smithsonite is a powerful stone which brings deep emotional healing. It soothes and calms the mind. It refreshes your emotional body and clears your mind when you get too involved in emotions which are suffocating you. It is considered to be a primarily emotional healer. Its frequency connects all chakras; it harmonizes your energy fields and releases you from anger. Smithsonite calms and relaxes your mind and heart, it expands your consciousness and allows you to enter into higher dimensions, it makes you more aware of your physical reality and makes you able to receive divine guidance in order to connect it with the material plane. It releases you from tensions and anxieties, it reminds you that you're not alone in this world, it helps you if you're feeling isolated or lonely. It brings you harmony and stability in relationships. It will protect you and keep you safe from a nervous breakdown if you're close to it, it will prevent the collapse of your being. It protects you from shocks and traumas, clears away the troubled past, and reminds you of universal love which exists all around you. It offers healing from childhood abuse or neglect if you went through any. It removes unpleasant emotions and reminds you of joyful feelings, peace, and compassion. It heals your heart in a physical and emotional sense, it heals from feelings of being abandoned or betrayed. It helps during meditation and it connects you with your higher self through awakening your psychic abilities.

Sugilite

Sugilite is a very powerful stone that brings wisdom and inspires true love within you. It awakens self-love and makes you fall in love with life. It connects you to deep vibrations of self-consciousness, it is a perfect stone for spiritual quest, it makes you feel alive, it changes your life and teaches you how to live your life. It gives you right directions and makes you choose wise options when you're indecisive. It is known as a "Love Stone"; its vibrations support spiritual development and bring you feelings of tenderness. It transforms your life and relationships in a gentle way, it encourages you to heal and forgive yourself and others. This crystal reminds you that you deserve love and that you are capable of feeling love and life. It encourages you to accept yourself totally, it will inspire your inner voice to speak up and turn to you, to come up on the surface and reveal the deep oceanic wisdom. It will open your eyes in a way that you can see the real you and meet yourself without any filters or masks. It cleanses and protects you from all the negative vibes around you on a daily basis. It is a great stone to meditate with and use during your dreams.

Diaspore

Diaspore fills your body with light, helping you remember your dreams and connecting you with the world of dreams, with experiences you go through while dreaming. It helps you find the meaning behind your dreams. It strengthens your life force and stimulates your mind. It helps with memory loss. It stimulates your crown chakra and it has grounding properties too. It helps you deal with life changes and challenges. It connects you to the higher-self and protects you during meditation. It brings you important answers about you and your life, it brings you better perception and clears the brain fog. It helps you remember things and it enhances your concentration and focus. It makes you feel strong and protected, it awakens true honesty and acceptance.

Diaspore brings you new visions and makes you more flexible, it makes you see others' points of view more easily. It makes you release painful past memories and communicate about negative experiences that you've been through. It opens you up to be more communicative and freer in self-expression. It enhances your mental power and releases you from stressful emotions and states. It is a pretty special stone, it is a chameleon stone, it displays different tones and it transforms its shade easily under different lights. It brings you enormous inspiration and creativity, it is especially helpful for poets, musicians, artists, dancers, all kinds of artistic talents which perfectly fits with your natural potential. It gives you persistence and the will to move forward.

African Turquoise

African turquoise is known as a "Stone of Evolution." Its high vibrations encourage you and rejuvenate your energy and life. It opens you for new experiences, it is a unique stone which makes you recognize the need and urge for self-development and metamorphosis. It is a stone of changes and transformations. It is called "turquoise" but it's actually a form of jasper. It supports you in making the necessary changes and modifications in your life, it helps you balance your past and future, it eases your struggles with yourself and others. It encourages growth and positive change, it inspires you for new experiences, new perceptions, new ideas and new possibilities, and it brings you new life.

African turquoise brings you great healing if you're fighting with depression, it makes you aware of your true purpose, and it leads you toward greater wisdom. It reminds you of the knowledge you already possess, it motivates you to become a better person in all aspects of your existence. It makes you see the brighter sides of life, it helps you if you're dealing with mood swings, it gives you strength and endurance for self-improvement, it brings you great confidence to pursue your goals and stay on track. This stone awakens your soul and makes you remember your source origins.

Aegirine

Aegirine is great for purification on all levels because it clears away toxic materials from your emotional, physical, and mental body, it creates an auric shield and removes negative attachments. It helps you "see the light" and turn away from negativity, it supports your skills and talents and makes you aware of your capabilities. It protects you from electromagnetic fields and helps to shift negative vibrations. It offers great release of emotional blockages, it brings you healing from addictions of all kinds: mental, emotional, substantial, or habitual. It can stimulate kundalini rising so you should be careful while using it. You should use it if you're already prepared with knowledge and experience to go through certain stages with yours and the collective unconscious.

Aegirine promotes integrity, growth, and a sense of purpose. It brings you a sense of nobility and encourages you to follow your heart. It connects you with the wisdom of Earth and the force of nature, it grounds you and protects you. It promotes confidence and it makes you willing to heal yourself from the inside. It helps you to prevent anxious attacks and transform inner insecurities into personal power. It eases and releases mental and emotional frustrations. It makes you feel more comfortable with yourself and others, it filters out negative energies, and motivates you to enter a state of emotional stability and harmony. It makes you seek for your own strength and security in order to make your life a true adventure of high quality.

Natrolite

Natrolite is also known as the "Stone of Angelic Realms." It has incredibly high vibrations and inspires you to look deep within yourself and ask for questions which could never occur to you before. It has an amazing energy and it helps you repair and recover broken parts of yourself. It provides personal and spiritual growth. It brings you alignment and connects you with higher spheres and higher chakras. It connects you with unseen and otherworldly existence and beings. It encourages you on your personal journey, it helps you open your inner gateways and pass through them steadily and fearlessly. It brings you deeper explorations, it pushes you toward enlightenment of hidden and forgotten inner chambers. It awakens exceptional self-healing abilities within you, it brings healing of past traumas, especially if you've been through or you're dealing with self-abusive tendencies.

Natrolite enhances your psychic abilities, it makes you more open for telepathic communication, inner guidance, and intuition. It harmonizes your nervous system. It is the perfect stone for transcendence and supports you immensely on your spiritual journey. It reminds you that you're the one who's in charge of your own life, it allows you to accept your own power and express the true you in the world. It protects you from damaging and destructive thoughts, emotions, actions, and words. It supports your independence in a healthy way, it motivates you to take full responsibility over your life and become the true example of growth and wisdom.

New and Full Moon Rituals Using Coral

Using coral during moon cycles is exceptionally good for you, dear Pisces. New and full moon energies can be transmuted and redirected towards desired goals and changes during rituals and mediations with your crystal. Coral and moon meditations can transform your whole life and personality for the better. This opens totally new doors of perception for you and makes you aware that you are truly a co-creator, that you really hold the power of creating your life. It will encourage you to take a risk and step out of your comfort zone, to do something unpredictable and unusual, to try something different and dive into deep waters of your being in order to cleanse, purify, transcend, and transform.

Being a Pisces and using coral during these phases of the moon will increase your potential and bring you insights about your true gifts and talents. Your natural abilities and qualities will come to light and your blockages and self-sabotaging patterns will too come to light so that you can see them, recognize them, acknowledge them, and heal what needs to be healed.

Before meditation you can cleanse and charge your crystal or do a ritual of holding it in your hands and doing conscious energy cleaning and charging. Burning sage is the safest way to cleanse your stone; run it through the smoke to purify it. You can also charge it under the moonlight. Coral is especially strong when it is charged under the full moonlight; it can be done two to three days before or after the full moon. Let your intuition guide you and choose what's the best for you.

New Moon

The new moon period should be used carefully and consciously; you should go through your wishes, passions, and desires to see what it is that you truly need. What is that one thing that is really necessary for you? Your intention is the most important thing during this phase of the moon because the emanations of the new moon are connected with humans' secret wants and needs, therefore, your intention plays the main role now and you should be careful that you're conscious of your intention and that it comes from the place of purity. Also, things that are behind this intention are very important and you should know what you want and make sure that what you sincerely want doesn't harm anyone. The new moon energy creates a pure magic for you and gives you what you need, it actually always gives you what you exactly need at that time and place. But when you consciously use this energy and meditate with your crystal energizing your intention, then you have an opportunity to become the one who's creating instead of mechanically surviving and letting things just happen to you without understanding and without the knowledge.

Find a nice and comfy place for you where you can be at peace with yourself, some place where you feel the least fear or possibly no fear at all, somewhere where you can relax completely. Find an enjoyable position for yourself, feel good in that position and don't start anything until you feel that that's it, that you feel good at your place and space. Wear your crystal or hold it in your hand. Close your eyes and take a deep breath, exhale through your mouth even deeper and longer if you can. Repeat this two more times; continue breathing normally. Feel the floor underneath you and your body on it, feel how connected you are with the earth, bring to consciousness this feeling of being attached to the ground. You are a water sign, but earth is also important for you; you need to feel safe, secure, and grounded in order to swim under deep oceanic waters and touch the untouchable. When you feel your connection with earth and ground, when you feel safe and secure enough, imagine being pulled deep down under the surface of existence, swim off through soft and silky waters. Feel the substance of this water, feel how it holds you and protects you, it is your shield and it covers you from every side, you are completely protected, this is your cradle and your womb. Feel the smoothness and warmth of being soaked in it, let it take you all the way down where it is dark and cold, but only until you get there.

Once you reach the dark and cold it won't feel that way, you will realize that it only seemed to be dark and cold from above, but now that you're there you actually feel like home. Meet all the creatures, see how much beauty lies under, feel this art of life through this world, feel connected with everything that you see. You're not afraid anymore, you see that things that frightened you were not to be feared at all, on the contrary, those things are your guides and helpers. You can detach from fearfully holding onto safety and comfort zones, you feel free for the first time in your life, you have personal freedom to be wherever you want to be, your self-confidence grows and you have courage to express yourself, you finally know what you want and what's missing. Set this intention and let it take you up on the surface again, fly off through the depths all the way up to the sun.

Feel every ray of the sun under water on your way back to the top, feel your inner light that you woke up during your meeting with the bottom, feel how your inner light and outer light meet each other and create more light, feel the unconditional love of nature and your surroundings. Feel how everything helps you and gives you needed food and drink. Feel your mother and father within you and around you, acknowledge how everything nurtures you and wants to take care of you. Take a deep breath when you reach the surface, lie down on the sea surface and just stay like that while feeling your intention strongly and being aware of the guidance of your coral and new moon energy. Be here and let the water take care of your intention and your life, be aware of your world which takes care of you, trust in it, put your trust in yourself and in all around you. When you're done, slowly open your eyes and stay with your eyes open for some time until you come back to this reality with your new experiences and wisdom.

New Moon Pisces Affirmations

I am free to be who I am supposed to be
I am responsible and I create my world and all the events in it
I am strong and decisive, and I know exactly what to do
when I need to do it
I am self-confident, and I am in charge of my life
I trust and I know that life gives me all that I need,
and everything is as it should be
I live in an abundant Universe, and I am a significant part of it
I allow the divine to work through me and bless me with its wisdom
I improve my life through every day
I am a creative soul, and I hold the keys of my destiny
I attract and allow true romance and love to visit me
I accept and embrace all the life's cycles that had to happen
and that will happen

Full Moon

The full moon is a highly charged period when you can heal your wounds and let your body, mind, and heart release from poisonous habits, addictions, thoughts, and emotions. This is a very intense phase where energy culminates and comes to the peak point, so it is very important that you take good care of what you're thinking, feeling, doing, saying, or not saying during this time. It is the perfect time to come to peace with yourself, to schedule this period for a self-date and dedicate your time and energy to self-development and self-healing. The full moon in general can be very tough for water signs and you're not an exception, since you easily absorb others' emotions. It is important then to be centered and aligned as much as you can during this time, which is why meditation with your crystal is a strong and powerful tool to help yourself and cleanse from anything that still blocks you or keeps you limited and unexpressive.

Find your sacred place for meditation, get yourself into a cozy and comfortable position, lie down or sit down. Before this you can make a little ritual and maybe dance or walk, sing, or do something dynamic that will discharge your physical tension, maybe some workout or yoga stretching. Anything that is your thing, anything that works as a stress relief and energizer for you.

So, when you find your best position and place, close your eyes and focus on your inhales and exhales. Imagine your symbol which represents two fish swimming in opposite directions, bound by silver cord. One is directed towards the bottom, the other is above the surface reaching up. As you inhale, imagine that you are a fish heading out towards the deep blue depths of an ocean, going inward, traveling to subconscious material, falling through the hole freely all the way to the most hidden memories and past lives. Take a deep breath and go as deep as your breath takes you, scan your past, let it show yourself to you, enlighten your unconscious parts—this is a chance to see them and take them out, transform or release them. As you exhale, imagine you're the other fish, the one which heads out towards the Universe and above the subconscious, above the water and its surface. You saw what is beneath the surface and now you're swimming to the sky, you are ready to release stuck memories, stories, images, relationships, attachments, emotions, thoughts, and habits. You release and transform. You go up and carry the wisdom from below. Continue doing this. Inhale—go all the way down, let your subconscious lead the way, let it guide you and show you where you're hurt, let it show you your wounds, your traumas, your pain, your sufferings, your ignorance, your attachments, your struggles, your deep issues that you couldn't recognize while you were floating on the surface, embrace them without fear, embrace them with forgiveness and nurturance.

As you exhale, take them out into the open, carry them to the top, let them dismantle and go where they need to go. You're awakening your symbol through this and making it purposeful. Let the two fish do their job with your conscious work and meditation. The full moon and crystal support what you're doing, especially while releasing and focusing on self-healing and cleansing from the destructive, negative, and victimized model of living. Inhale, collect your burdens, collect your pains, collect your despair and helplessness, collect your past lives and childhood memories. Exhale, let them come up, release them, take them to the surface, let them return to their source, there's no need to hold them anymore.

You understand that you were the one who kept yourself imprisoned, now you're releasing and liberating all these sedimented memories and emotions that kept you locked and that you locked within yourself. You didn't even know that you had this inside of you, you weren't even aware of what's hiding beneath your surface, you don't even remember when it happened or why or how, it doesn't even matter. All that matters is that you're here now. You're remembering who you are, that you're enlightening your subconscious. Continue this process as long as you

196

feel the need to do it. Feel how it eases you, feel how it unburdens you and makes you feel lighter. Slowly open your eyes when you finish, stay with yourself, give yourself a smile, thank yourself for everything, forgive yourself for everything, love yourself, show kindness to yourself.

You can use a journal to write down your experience and feelings after this meditation. You might want to draw or paint your experience, or maybe turn it into poetry or create music. Use your creativity and artistic inner genius to express what you've been through. Feel free to share your experience and go back to it anytime you feel let down, betrayed, alone, sad, fearful, angry, confused, or any hardening feeling and emotion that comes to you. Remember that there's a sanctuary within you, there's a field that you have access to all the time, no matter what, you just have to enter it with your clean thoughts and clear heart.

Full Moon Pisces Affirmations

I allow the Universe to guide me
I let myself to be in peace
I am highly intuitive, and I follow my intuition
I am connected with the whole world,
and I am never divided or separate
I am thankful for all the sorrows, griefs, turmoils,
obstacles, confusions, and challenges,
and I am thankful for the wisdo
and knowledge they brought to me
I am an eternal being of light, and I never disappear
I am here since forever, always have been and always will be
I am embraced and loved by the Divine Mother and Divine Father
I am grateful for all the hard lessons in my life
for they have taught me in the most meaningful and essential way
I celebrate this life and I welcome all the new adventures
and ups and downs that come along with it